With best wishes
Lady Bird Johnson

The President's Lady

The
PRESIDENT'S LADY

An Intimate Biography of
Mrs. Lyndon B. Johnson

BY

MARIE SMITH

with a Foreword by
Former President HARRY S TRUMAN

Random House New York

FIRST PRINTING

 Published in New York by Random House, Inc., and simultaneously in Toronto, Canada, by Random House of Canada Limited.

Library of Congress Catalog Card Number: 64-17940

Excerpt on page 167 from an article by Mrs. Lyndon B. Johnson, *The Washington Post*, April 10, 1961. Reprinted by permission.

MANUFACTURED IN THE UNITED STATES OF AMERICA BY

The Haddon Craftsmen, Scranton, Pa.

Typography by Tere LoPrete

Foreword

A President needs many things. I can speak with authority because I've been one.

Brains, ability, a loyal following mean nothing unless—by his side—there is an intelligent and understanding wife.

Again, I speak with authority. Because I have one.

And for these two reasons I am delighted to write the foreword to Miss Smith's book about the First Lady whom I have known in person and in deed for more than twenty years.

I had the pleasure of meeting Mrs. Lyndon B. Johnson when she was the wife of a young enthusiastic Congressman from Texas; of knowing her even better as her husband rose to become a United States Senator, Majority Leader of his Party, and Vice-President of the United States.

Last March I accompanied her to Greece on her first mission abroad as First Lady—to represent her husband at the funeral of King Paul.

One has only to watch her in action to see why he would not hesitate to give her this—and other—assignments. She is a real human being. She is a selfless human being. She knows what the business of government is all about.

I am delighted that such an able reporter as Marie Smith, who has known the Johnsons through the many milestones of their career, has written a book to help more people meet our First Lady. They have a real treat in store.

Harry S Truman

Harry Truman

Contents

The President's Lady

[I]

A New Role—How It Began

Lady Bird Johnson was proud of Dallas that warm sunny Friday morning, November 22, 1963, as she rode through the familiar streets lined with cheering crowds turned out to welcome their President. The city's political climate was unpredictable, but today it was warm and friendly and she was happy. She could remember another day, though, when it had been cold and hostile, but that was in 1960, when she and her husband were campaigning for the Kennedy-Johnson ticket in the presidential election.

That ticket had, indeed, won and President John F. Kennedy was now in Dallas to greet the citizens and address a luncheon at the Trade Mart, sponsored by the Dallas Citizens Council, the Dallas Assembly, and the

Graduate Research Center of the Southwest. No one could accurately predict how this city with its shifting political sentiments—sometimes Democratic, sometimes Republican, but strongly conservative—would react to a Democratic President it had not supported in the 1960 election. But this day it seemed the past was forgotten, and thousands of friendly faces smiled as they cheered him on the long ten-mile motorcade trip from Love Field to the Dallas Trade Mart. Riding with the President in his special limousine—with the protective glass bubble removed so he could see and be more easily seen—was Mrs. Kennedy in a cheery pink suit. She smiled and waved at the crowds, who shouted her name as the motorcade slowly rolled by. With the presidential couple, on seats in front, were Texas Governor and Mrs. John B. Connally. They were also smiling and happy at the obviously warm welcome.

Two cars behind, with only a Secret Service car between them, rode the Vice-President of the United States, Lyndon B. Johnson, a native Texan, and his Texas-born wife, Lady Bird. With them was Senator Ralph Yarborough, also of Texas. There were cheers for them too—and Lady Bird held an arm bouquet of yellow roses, the flower that had almost become her trademark in her travels. It had been presented to her on arrival at Love Field, at the same time Mrs. Kennedy was given a bouquet of red roses.

For eight miles they rode through the crowd-lined streets in the warm, almost hot, noonday sun, seeing thousands of friendly faces. Mrs. Johnson scanned them to see if she might recognize some special friends, because she had many in Dallas. She had gone to junior college there for two years, and had been there innumerable times since to shop and visit. The city held many memories for her.

Suddenly, over the cheers and applause, three shots rang out in rapid-fire succession. For one fleeting second

Lady Bird thought that it was the backfire of a motorcycle, because there were so many around—in front of the motorcade and flanking the presidential car to the rear—or that perhaps it was a firecracker shot off by someone to match the mood of the great gala day it had been from the start.

Then she heard a sharp command coming over the limousine's intercom system from the lead car: "Let's get out of here!" The presidential car moved ahead with frightening speed; for another fleeting second she thought, or hoped, that maybe this was because they were thirty minutes behind schedule and were hurrying to get on to the luncheon. But just as the car lurched forward, Rufus Youngblood, the Secret Service agent who was the Vice-President's personal bodyguard, vaulted from the front to the rear seat, pushed her husband to the floor and fell on top of him. He gave her and Senator Yarborough a sharp command: "Get down!" For a bare fraction of a second, subconsciously, she thought that this was not the way Youngblood normally talked. She knew him as the politest of gentlemen, always saying "please." But this time he shouted the command as if he were the boss, and at that moment he was. Obediently she and Senator Yarborough bent down from the waist in order to get below the window level of the open limousine.

In this position they sped through the streets for five minutes—where to, she knew not. Then the driver slammed on the brakes so hard that the car careened around a corner and stopped short at a building. She cautiously looked up to see where they were. Her eyes fastened on a sign: "Parkland Hospital." "I knew then it was something bad," she recalls.

She watched with almost frozen unbelief as stretcher-bearers came out and carried the limp body of President Kennedy from his car into the hospital. Mrs. Kennedy walked at his side. Another stretcher brought Texas Governor Connally into the hospital and his wife followed. The Vice-President strode in behind them, and she and Senator Yarborough followed. While her husband was spirited into one room under Secret Service protection, she, escorted by Senator Yarborough and Texas Congressman Jack Brooks, went in search of Mrs. Kennedy and Mrs. Connally.

They found Mrs. Kennedy first, standing dazed in a corridor outside an emergency room in which doctors worked swiftly over her husband. Already Mrs. Kennedy knew the truth. She had seen the horrible damage of the bullet that struck her husband's head, she had held the silent lifeless form on that nightmare ride to the hospital. But Mrs. Johnson did not know. She still hoped for the best. Lady Bird walked toward Mrs. Kennedy, her arms outstretched in compassion to offer what consolation she could. Too stunned for tears, Mrs. Kennedy's only words were: "At least we had ten years together." She repeated them again, clinging to this thought as her only consolation in those first moments of realization that her husband was gone.

Lady Bird, still unaware that the President was dead or dying, left Senator Yarborough with Mrs. Kennedy and went on with Jack Brooks in search of Nellie Connally. After what seemed an almost endless stroll down winding corridors and up flights of stairs, she found her. The two women, who had been friends—close friends—for thirty years, fell into each other's arms and dissolved their anguish in tears. At that moment, neither knew whether Governor Connally would live or not.

A few moments later Lady Bird returned to her husband and it was then that she learned the truth. She heard White House Associate Press Secretary Malcolm Kilduff address her husband as "Mr. President." Her first reaction when she realized that President Kennedy had been slain was a feeling of incredulity, then anger. Then a great compassion for her husband welled up within her—the weight of the load that was falling on him became apparent to her at that moment. And her heart ached for the women whose husbands had been struck down by the then unknown assassin's bullets—but not once did it occur to her what it would all mean to her personally. That came later, hours later—after she had returned to her home in Washington.

Now they had to arrange for the return to Washington, but her husband, the new President, who had not yet been sworn in, said they would wait until the cars were closed up before they left the hospital for the airport. Then he got into one car, surrounded by Secret Service agents, and Lady Bird got into another. As they started to pull away from the hospital, Lady Bird motioned through the window for Elizabeth Carpenter, who was then executive assistant to the Vice-President, and Marie Fehmer, his secretary, to follow them. The two girls climbed into a police car and followed the two limousines to Love Field. The new President was to take the oath of office in the plane, but they had to await the arrival of two persons. Federal Judge Sarah T. Hughes, a longtime friend of the Johnsons', had been summoned to administer the oath; and Mrs. Kennedy had said she wanted to be there to witness the transfer of the office from her husband to his successor.

At 2:38 P.M. Central Standard Time, less than two hours after Mr. Kennedy died, the tall Texan was sworn in as the nation's thirty-sixth President. He stood in the crowded, gold-upholstered cabin of *Air Force One*, the presidential plane, and repeated the oath after Judge Hughes. His hand was placed on an old leather-bound Bible that was kept in the President's compartment of the plane. Mrs. Kennedy stood at his left and Lady Bird at his right.

There were tears in the Judge's eyes and her voice

sometimes faltered as she administered the oath, the first woman ever to administer the oath of office to a President of the United States. Mr. Johnson repeated each word clearly: "I do solemnly swear that I will faithfully execute the office of President of the United States, and will to the best of my ability protect and defend the Constitution of the United States. So help me God."

After the last word he turned and kissed Lady Bird on the forehead. Then both turned to Mrs. Kennedy. Lady Bird clasped her hands. "The whole nation mourns your husband," Lady Bird said, her first utterance as the nation's thirty-second First Lady.

Later Mrs. Kennedy returned to the rear compartment, where her husband's body rested in a casket. She sat at his side through most of the two-and-a-half-hour flight to Washington. Lady Bird sat beside her husband for a while, then went back to comfort Mrs. Kennedy. When she returned to the President, he placed a call over the plane's telephone to Mrs. Joseph P. Kennedy, the slain President's mother. He was like a man in anguish as he spoke to her. "I wish to God there was something I could do," he said and then, as if he could go no further, added quickly, "Here's Lady Bird." He thrust the telephone into her hands. Completely without time to think about what she was going to say, Lady Bird began: "Mrs. Kennedy, we feel as though our heart is cut out, but we must remember how fortunate our country was to have your son as long as it did. Our love and our prayers are with you." The sorrowful seventy-two-year-old mother said simply, "Thank you, Lady Bird."

President Johnson telephoned Mrs. Connally also; then he turned his thoughts to setting down a statement to the American people. With Lady Bird next to him, he consulted her regarding his choice of words as he composed the speech. Immediately on landing in Washington at Andrews Air Force Base, he said:

"This is a sad time for all people. We have suffered a loss that cannot be weighed. For me, it is a deep personal tragedy. I know that the world shares the sorrow that Mrs. Kennedy and her family bear. I will do my best. That is all I can do. I ask your help and God's."

He repeated the statement on the White House lawn, where his helicopter landed in the glare of spotlights. Together he and Lady Bird walked to the steps outside the slain President's office. There they parted. Lady Bird, accompanied by Elizabeth Carpenter, got into a limousine and rode to her home, The Elms, while the new President went to his vice-presidential office in the nearby Executive Office Building.

At The Elms, Lady Bird found a crowd—newspaper reporters, photographers, neighbors and curious sympathizers—clustered around the tall iron gates. The reporters asked her for a statement. Once inside, she quickly and quietly composed one. Mrs. Carpenter jotted it down and relayed it to the press. It said: "The way I feel, it has all been a dreadful nightmare; somehow we must find the strength to go on."

Lucy Baines, the Johnsons' sixteen-year-old daughter, had come home from National Cathedral School and was waiting at the door for her mother. Crushed, too, under the sorrowful events, she, like so many others, tried to find something good to say in the sad crisis. She said, "Oh, Mother, I go to a wonderful school. They called me into the office and told me, then everybody went to the gymnasium to pray for my father." She was in tears.

Lynda Bird, their nineteen-year-old daughter, who was a sophomore at the University of Texas, heard the news on the campus, and promptly went to the Governor's mansion to be with and comfort the children of Governor and Mrs. Connally. At that time they did not know whether their father would live or not. Lady Bird was impressed by this spontaneous thoughtfulness and compassion of her elder daughter and it was the brightest spot in that dark hour.

That evening at The Elms she watched how televison was still trying to piece together a lot of probable facts, and when the President came home late that night, they sat together in quiet solemnity watching the television reports of the day's tragic events.

Dressed in black, Lady Bird was at her husband's side the next morning as he led Cabinet members and their wives to the bier of the slain President in the black-crepe-shrouded East Room of the the White House. She went with him to the second floor to see Mrs. Kennedy, and told the former First Lady she could remain in the mansion as long as she wished. For the next three days, Lady Bird was a picture of quiet, calm dignity as she, in public and private, took care of the things that needed to be done. At The Elms a flood of letters and telegrams from all over the country came in, offering condolences, prayers and good wishes.

She accepted the assistance of Senate wives and close friends in sorting, reading and replying to the messages. She went with her husband on Sunday morning to St. Mark's Episcopal Church on Capitol Hill, which she had attended since she came to Washington as a congressman's wife twenty-six years earlier, and side by side they knelt in prayer. After church they attended the coffee hour in the parish house and greeted some two hundred members of the congregation. She went with the President to the White House to ride with Mrs. Kennedy behind the horse-drawn caisson that carried the slain President's body to the Capitol for repose in the Rotunda; she was with him again on Monday as the caisson returned the flag-draped casket to the White House, and from there she walked beside him in the procession behind the artillery caisson proceeding to St. Matthew's Cathedral; she was also at his side on the hour-long ride to Arlington National Cemetery for the interment.

From the cemetery, Lady Bird returned home alone to give way to her weariness and grief. But there was not even time for that. In the State Department's reception rooms her husband was greeting the scores of foreign leaders who had flown to Washington from all parts of the globe to pay their respects to the dead President. It was expected to be an all-male function, but there were several women among the dignitaries: Queen Frederika of Greece; Madame Pandit, India's delegate to the United Nations; Golda Meir, Israel's Minister of Foreign Affairs, and Princess Beatrix of the Netherlands. So while she was having dinner from a tray at home, a surprise telephone call came from her husband asking her to come and join him. "You can sit in the corner and talk to the ladies," he told her.

Lady Bird responded quickly, and a few minutes later was on the spot talking to the ladies and greeting other world leaders. She stayed for fifty minutes, as long as the women guests were there, then she left her husband to continue his duties alone.

Lady Bird Johnson awoke the next morning to a full realization of her new role as First Lady. She had to prepare for the move to the White House. Early that morning J. B. West, chief usher at the White House, arrived at the Johnson home and spent two hours showing her floor plans of the Executive Mansion. From the plans, she tentatively selected the rooms that would be used by various members of her family. That afternoon she went to the White House, where Mrs. Kennedy briefed her on the domestic details of running the White House. For an hour and a half they conferred, and Lady Bird met many members of the staff and talked over the logistics of housekeeping in so large a home. If she had any fears about stepping into the role of chatelaine of the Executive Mansion no one knew it, for she did not complain or seem overwhelmed at the future before her. Her main thoughts were still for Mrs. Kennedy. Again, she asked her to remain there until she had had time to wind up her affairs at her convenience. She also invited Mrs. Kennedy to continue using the third-floor solarium for Caroline Kennedy's nursery school as long as she wished, and Mrs. Kennedy accepted the offer for the period remaining until the end of the year.

In the meantime, Lady Bird kept busy with her family, and answering the telegrams and letters that continued to flow in. She also took time out to read the various drafts of her husband's first address to a joint session of Congress. And the next day, a Wednesday, she was in the front row of the executive gallery in the House of Representatives to hear him deliver it. With her were family members, close personal friends and political friends. There were Lynda Bird and Lucy Baines; Mrs. William White, wife of the syndicated columnist and a long-time friend; Roxanne George, of Mattoon, Illinois, a niece of the President's; Georgia Governor Carl Sanders; Chicago Mayor Richard Daley; Director of the Peace Corps Sargent Shriver; Arthur Schlesinger, Jr., President Kennedy's special assistant; former Pennsylvania Governor David Lawrence; New York Mayor Robert Wagner; Houston Harte, publisher of the San Angelo (Texas) *Standard-Times;* Mrs. Horace Busby, wife of one of the President's assistants; Mrs. Donald MacArthur, Mrs. Johnson's niece; Harry Provence, publisher of the Waco (Texas) *News Tribune.*

Although she had read it earlier, Lady Bird was moved by the speech that was interrupted thirty-two times by applause. And she was proud of the manner in which her husband delivered it. "It was an anguished spot for him to be in," she said. "But the speech was great and I have great faith."

On Saturday, December 7, 1963, Lady Bird Johnson took up residence in the White House. Already she was beginning to feel the responsibilities of her new role as First Lady, but it was when she moved into the 163-year-old official residence that she began to feel her place in history.

One of the first things she did was go around and meet everyone who worked at the White House—from the kitchen maids to the bouquet-makers in the flower room. She asked chief usher J. B. West to take her through the mansion, from top to bottom, and to each employee she expressed her sympathy on the sad departure of the Kennedy family, and told them what kind of people the Johnsons were and how they lived. Another thing she did was begin the first in a series of "educational" tours of the 132-room mansion. She called on the curator, James Ketchum, as her guide for these. "I don't want to live in a house that is unknown to me," she said. "I knew all about The Brick House in which I was born in East Texas, and I want to know all about this one." This was a project she went about slowly, because she wanted to make the study in depth rather than skim the surface and maybe never get back to the details.

The biggest challenge Lady Bird had to face as the days went by was to find courage, she said, "to stanchly say no to enough things to save out time for Lyndon, Lynda Bird and Lucy Baines, at the expense of draining yourself to say no to something you like. The core of the whole thing is what, with the amount of hours, energy and brains you have got, you can do that will accomplish the most."

There were many things she wanted to do, things she

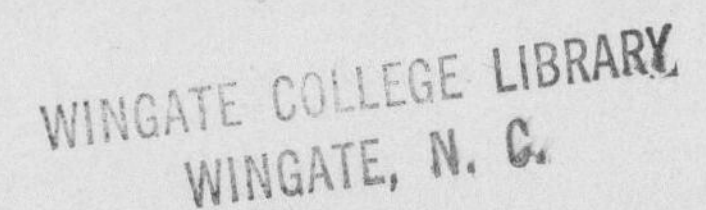

was interested in, things she wanted to learn more about, but where would she find the time? Always an avid reader, during the first two months she lived in the White House she did not read a single book. "I've got to work book-reading back into my schedule," she declared.

Her days were now beginning to shape into their present pattern. In the mornings, the first thing she does after an eight o'clock or eight-thirty breakfast is to consult with three of her staff members: Ashton Gonella, her personal secretary, who has an office on the third floor; Bess Abell, her former personal secretary, who is now White House social secretary; and Elizabeth Carpenter, her staff director and press secretary.

Lady Bird dictates answers to her mail and sometimes signs as many as two hundred letters; she makes decisions on state dinners in the planning stage, invitations she will accept, luncheons she is planning; she works all morning to clear her desk of the dozen of things that have piled up in the preceding twenty-four hours. Sometimes as she works, with her shoes off for comfort, her husband comes in with two, three or more of his VIP callers brought over from his office to show them the family's private quarters and to meet Lady Bird.

She converted the small corner room, which her predecessor had used as a dressing room, into an office, and set her desk across the window so that she looks out on the Washington Monument as she works. There are also a chaise lounge and bookcases. "That little room has just one door and I close that one and do a lot of my work in there," she said recently.

At noon, she often gives a luncheon for ladies, sometimes is hostess to luncheon guests her husband has invited; or while he entertains a stag group in the family dining room, she may lunch from a tray with a friend, or someone with whom she needs to confer, in the Queen's Sitting Room at the east end of the hall, but only after she has first greeted and welcomed her husband's guests. Lady Bird is a gracious hostess who knows just what to say to make each guest feel wanted and at home.

She tries to save some time for herself in the afternoon, for appointments with an interior decorator on fixing up Lynda's and Lucy's rooms, for example, or to attend to personal matters pertaining to the children or the family. When Lucy comes home from school she spends some time with her—the mother-and-daughter ties are very strong—and she sandwiches in between all these things some of her "must" reading. These are reports from the State Department on foreign visitors who are expected, facts about the political and economic conditions in their countries, and a lot of other memoranda that a First Lady must know about the operation of the White House and things she should know as the President's wife, such as her husband's schedule and the guests he has invited to breakfast the next day. Added to all this is the fact she is always on call when the President wants her to come to his office to meet one of his visitors.

Lady Bird has set aside an hour each day for recording her life in the White House. She does not write it in a diary, but talks into a tape recorder about the things she is doing, her impressions and feelings as she lives each day in the house of history. She began it immediately, the day after she became First Lady, starting with the nightmarish experience in Dallas. She is not sure what she will do with her personal history. She says only that she is doing it for her children, and the grandchildren she hopes to have; that it is much too personal to let anyone else see or hear it now. But there are hopes around the White House that some day she might permit it to be published.

There are no office hours for a First Lady and her day

is not done with the beginning of the five o'clock traffic exodus from Washington to the suburbs. There may be a cocktail-hour staff conference, or a meeting with some group which has asked to see the President on a specific matter; or if he is working late at his office, she will walk over—through the long corridor and covered portico—about seven o'clock "to hold his hand," as she puts it. Sometimes he returns to the mansion with her for dinner. Other times, there may be guests for dinner. Rare is the evening that the Johnsons dine alone, because they are experts at mixing business, pleasure and entertaining.

Often the President works until midnight and beyond, and since Lady Bird requires more sleep than he does, she will excuse herself from the yellow-walled Oval Room where he holds his evening sessions until all hours, and retire.

During the first month in the White House, Lady Bird returned almost daily to The Elms and spent three hours there each time, sorting things that were to be stored, sent to the ranch in Texas, or sold with the house. She was also trying to add touches of home to the White House, which, without them, seemed large, impersonal and like a grand hotel despite the attractive improvements and extensive redecorating and upgrading made by Mrs. Kennedy. Lady Bird brought her Lowestoft china for the shelves in the family sitting room, the yellow Oval Room (a formal drawing room) and the great reception hall. She also brought her collection of Dorothy Doughty porcelain birds and scattered them on shelves and what-nots as bright homey touches, and paintings by Texas artist Porfirio Salinas of the hill country from which they came were hung on the walls of the bedroom she and the President share.

It is the same bedroom that was occupied by Abraham Lincoln when he was President, and by President and Mrs. Kennedy. One of the final things Mrs. Kennedy did before leaving the White House was to have inscribed this historic footnote on the white marble mantel: "In this room lived John Fitzgerald Kennedy with his wife Jacqueline—during the two years, ten months and two days he was President of the United States. January 20, 1961—November 22, 1963." It is directly below another inscription on the mantel that reads: "In this room Abraham Lincoln slept during his occupancy of the White House as President of the United States. March 4, 1861—April 13, 1865."

Few women would envy Lady Bird her role as First Lady succeeding the brilliant, beautiful Jacqueline Kennedy, who during her occupancy of the White House filled it with her own gaiety, glamor and grace. Mrs. Kennedy had sparked an interest in the historic mansion unequaled by any of her predecessors; she formed a Fine Arts Committee for the White House to replace the heterogeneous collection of furniture with authentic late-eighteenth- and early-nineteenth-century pieces by some of America's finest craftsmen. From all over the country historic and beautiful antiques were donated, making the rooms already steeped in history actually come alive for the thousands who went through the state rooms each day they were open to the public; she and her husband sparked a renaissance in art and culture by their own interest in music, theater, ballet, paintings and literature. She even made White House news by hiring a French chef to spruce up the food served at state dinners as well as family meals.

Lady Bird had no thought of competing with or seeking to exceed the accomplishments of her predecessor, when she became First Lady. She planned to carry on the projects initiated by Mrs. Kennedy but not to imitate her. She had great appreciation for all the First Ladies who had served before her, but she did not plan to emulate the life of any one. She wanted to be herself, and set her own pattern. She has a deep political awareness and a social consciousness that makes her sensitive to the needs of humanity that may well point the way to her greatest activity as First Lady. At any rate, before she had been in the White House long, it became apparent that a strong, warm, outgoing personality was hostess in the nation's Executive Mansion, and that she, as First Lady, would write her chapter in history in her own unique way.

[II]

Stepping Stones

A few days after she became First Lady, Mrs. Johnson confided to a close friend: "I feel as if I am suddenly on stage for a part I never rehearsed."

It was a gross understatement of her preparedness for the role, however, for Lady Bird Johnson was better qualified by background, experience and knowledge for the role of First Lady than had been any of her thirty-one predecessors.

This dark-haired brown-eyed Texas beauty brought to the White House a native charm for winning friends, a shrewd brain for business, a deft touch for diplomacy, and a persuasiveness in politics, all qualities which her predecessors had possessed in greater or lesser measure.

But more importantly, what she had that none of her

predecessors had had to the same or nearly equal degree was twenty-seven years of experience on the national political scene and a personal insight into how government operates in Washington. During these years she was not only wife and confidante but also full political partner to her husband, who rose from congressional secretary to member of Congress, serving twelve years in the House of Representatives, twelve years in the Senate (of which he was Majority Leader for six years), and almost three years as Vice-President before he became President.

Mrs. Kennedy had been a senator's wife for seven years when she moved into the White House and before that she had gone to school and worked in Washington, and Mrs. Truman's husband had been senator for ten years and Vice-President for a few months before he succeeded to the Presidency, but their experience did not equal Mrs. Johnson's long experience on the political scene. And Eleanor Roosevelt, to whom Mrs. Johnson is often compared for her humanitarian interests and political awareness, had lived in Washington only as wife of the Secretary of the Navy before she moved into the White House, although she had long been politically active in New York, where her husband had been governor. Other First Ladies had also lived in Washington while their husbands served in Congress, but none as long as Mrs. Johnson.

From the very beginning, when she came to Washington as a bride in 1934 at the age of twenty-one, Lady Bird Johnson had been close to the center of power in both the executive and legislative branches of government. Through what she likes to call "those yeasty years" of Roosevelt activity she was more aware than most women, or even men, of the New Deal that President Franklin Delano Roosevelt was offering the country and of his strategy for putting his program forward, for her husband was a Roosevelt protégé. He had campaigned and been elected as a Roosevelt supporter in 1937. The handbill for his first campaign in Texas' sprawling ten-county Tenth District had cited this as one of his merits, plus the fact that he was "big enough for the job, young enough to get it done"—and a man with a "dynamic personality" who knew Washington and could "get things done for the district."

During those years Mrs. Johnson went to her first White House reception, given by President and Mrs. Roosevelt for members of Congress and their wives. Her husband was also a frequent guest at the White House and came home telling her about conferring with the President as he worked in bed with a blue cape around his shoulders. Lyndon Johnson often said that President Roosevelt "was just like a father to me," and he got to know the important figures in the Roosevelt Administration—a relationship that made it easier for him to keep his campaign promise to "get things done for my district."

The Johnsons' own home was a gathering place for politicians who had arrived and those on their way up. One of the closest and most frequent guests was the late Speaker of the House Sam Rayburn, who took young Lyndon Johnson under his wing in the House and trained him for leadership. Rayburn and Johnson's father, Samuel Ealy Johnson, Jr., had served together in the Texas State Legislature and were close friends. When the two men—Sam Rayburn and Lyndon—talked politics at her dinner table, Lady Bird listened intently, absorbing and digesting all she heard. Later she was able to discuss politics with Lyndon and give her own views on the matters, views that he found remarkably sound. He listened to her then, and he still does.

Although the Johnsons were very close to the Trumans, there were fewer visits to the White House during the Truman years. The reason was that President Truman and his family lived for many months of his administration in Blair House, across Pennsylvania Avenue from the White House, and did limited entertaining there. The Executive Mansion had been quietly decaying from age on the inside and no one recognized the extent of the damage until one day Margaret Truman's piano leg sank through a board on the second floor of the mansion. That called for immediate action, so the entire house was gutted and repaired while Mr. Truman was President.

When President Eisenhower took up residence in the rebuilt mansion in 1953, the social season opened in full swing—there were receptions, state dinners, luncheons—and Senator Lyndon Johnson, who by this time had risen to the position of Majority Leader in the Senate, and his Lady Bird were frequently on the guest list.

Then during the two years and ten months her husband was Vice-President, Lady Bird was not only a guest at almost every state dinner and reception President and Mrs. Kennedy gave, she found herself acting as White House hostess on many occasions. She became as familiar with the state rooms of the White House as with her own home. "Yet," she confesses, "to me it is always a great thrill to walk into that stately gold and white dining room and see the brooding picture of Lincoln looking down sternly from the mantelpiece and read the prayerful quotation from John Adams in 1800: 'I pray heaven to bestow the best of blessings on this house and on all that shall hereafter inhabit it. May none but honest and wise men ever rule under this roof.' "

When she became Second Lady in January of 1961, Mrs. Johnson set herself three duties: "To help Lyndon all I can; to lend a hand to Mrs. Kennedy when she needs me; and to be a more alive me." She carried out all three—and the first two with such frequency that she soon became known as Washington's number one pinch hitter.

If Lyndon Johnson had promised to attend a gathering—social or political—and found he could not make it, he sent his best substitute, his wife. Once he was to speak at a Detroit political rally for Michigan Governor John Swainson during the 1962 campaign. At the last minute he telephoned his wife. "Go ahead, Lady Bird," he said, "I can't leave Washington." It turned out to be a critical day in the Cuban crisis. He asked her to do what she could to make up for his absence, and she did. She stepped before the audience in the huge auditorium, apologized for her husband and explained his absence. Then she gave a stirring political speech, got down from the rostrum and shook hands with all of the five hundred people present.

She substituted for Mrs. Kennedy on numerous occasions, giving herself training for the job that was soon to be her own. In the summer of 1962, while Mrs. Kennedy was vacationing in Newport, Rhode Island, Mrs. Johnson was one of three hostesses she designated as her stand-in at a White House reception for wives of delegates to an international monetary conference. In the spring of 1963, after Mrs. Kennedy canceled her official engagements to await the birth of a baby expected in August, Mrs. Johnson served as hostess at the luncheon President Kennedy gave at the White House for Crown Princess Beatrix, heiress to the Dutch throne; and again in May of that year she substituted for Mrs. Kennedy at a White House luncheon for Senate wives.

As a pinch hitter, Lady Bird knew her job and she did it well. Often she stepped in on short notice and rearranged her own plans to lighten the load on Mrs. Kennedy. She always stayed in the background to let the full spotlight fall on the First Lady. One day in May of 1962 she was to be merely a guest at a dinner that evening at which the Vice-President would receive the second annual Peace Through Health Award. But her plans were sharply altered by a telephone call from the White House. It was

Pierre Salinger, President Kennedy's press secretary, telling her that that night Mrs. Kennedy was to be given the TV Emmy Award for Public Service for her televised tour of the White House, and couldn't make it. Would Mrs. Johnson receive it for her?

Lady Bird said yes. She quickly shifted her plans, met Lyndon at his dinner, explained that she would have to leave the head table briefly. When the time came she did, took a cab to a nearby hotel, stepped into a phone booth and composed her acceptance speech, then went to the banquet hall to face the VIP audience and the TV cameras for a nation-wide broadcast. Paying tribute to Mrs. Kennedy, she ended her remarks with these words: "If all history lessons could be presented against such a background and by such a teacher, I am sure the entire nation would be eager to go back to school." Mrs. Johnson did not linger for the applause; she returned to the dinner to witness the presentation to her husband and to join in the applause for him.

Jacqueline Kennedy was grateful to Mrs. Johnson for her help and support when she was First Lady, and after Lady Bird moved into the White House as her successor, Mrs. Kennedy said, "Mrs. Johnson is wonderful . . . she is always so generous with her time and willing to be of help."

Until her husband sought the presidential nomination in 1960 and, having failed to achieve that, was nominated for the Vice-Presidency by the Democratic National Convention, few people outside official government circles in Washington and the people of Texas knew Lady Bird Johnson. But then, like a Texas tornado she whipped across the national landscape—seeking votes for the Kennedy-Johnson ticket.

The impact she made was reflected in the newspaper

headlines she made across the country. Therein lay the answer to the often-asked question: "What is Lady Bird Johnson like?"

A Phoenix newspaper called her "a real love" with "charm as big as Arizona," and the thing that impressed those who met her in Spokane, Washington, was her "keen appreciation of the average person."

"Lady Bird Johnson's biggest asset is that she is an intelligent and articulate businesswoman," observed the New York *World-Telegram and Sun*, and in Indianapolis the words were "charming, pretty, vivacious, happy." "The way the home folks phrase it, 'she rings true,' " said the Dallas *Morning News*, and the Atlanta *Constitution* described her as "one of those people who would have made a success in almost any field."

"She is a gal with gumption," said the *Daily Oklahoman*. "Although frightened of the public forum, she took a public-speaking course to steel herself to face audiences. Timid with firearms, she nevertheless learned to shoot several years ago and now handles a .28 shotgun in the Texas dove season and a rifle for the November-December deer season."

Helen Thomas, Washington reporter for United Press International, observed that "Mrs. Johnson is setting a pace for herself reminiscent in some ways of the late beloved Eleanor Roosevelt. In elite and affluent Washington circles, official wives are apt to forget the less fortunate people in other areas. But Lady Bird Johnson remembers them. She has brought a warm and human touch to the Kennedy New Frontier. Though her knees knock with stage fright at times, she forces herself to accept many of the speaking invitations that pour in on her."

Another Washington reporter, Frances Lide of the *Evening Star*, said: "Her soft drawl and the name Lady Bird may conjure up an aura of leisure and magnolia blossoms. But the gentle manner of Mrs. Lyndon B. Johnson masks stamina, efficiency and a strong sense of purpose. She is feminine, friendly and folksy, as she has proved on the campaign trail. She is eloquent too and never more so than when she is stirred by the challenges of citizenship. 'In the space age,' she says, 'passive citizenship is a luxury no one can afford.' "

Frances Lewine of Associated Press assessed her this way: "Lady Bird Johnson is philosophical and thoughtful about her role—searching for the significant, and ever mindful that 'it takes a firm set of values and great discipline in Washington or you find yourself frittering away sixteen hours a day over trivia, cups of tea and light comment.' "

The picture of Lady Bird Johnson emerges even more clearly through the words of those who knew her well when she was a congressional wife.

They see her as quiet and responsive to her duties. One friend said, "She has the touch of velvet and the stamina of steel." Another: "I have never known a more disciplined woman. Through self-discipline, she has acquired self-mastery." "She is warm, intuitive, thoughtful of everyone else, and has a poetic way of speaking," said another friend, and a Senate wife adds, "She never loses her temper and never loses a friend. I can't recall a time when Bird lost her disposition and I have seen her under some tough pressures." Another friend said, "When you try to describe her, she turns out sounding too good to be true—but she is like that."

This is the woman who today occupies the White House as the nation's thirty-second First Lady.

One unexpected decision Lady Bird had to face when her husband became President was what she should be called. In recent years, other First Ladies had been called by their given names: Jacqueline Kennedy, Mamie Eisenhower, Bess Truman, Eleanor Roosevelt—always with the prefix title of First Lady. Reporters and writers found it clumsy to say "First Lady Lady Bird Johnson" so they besieged her with questions about what they should call her: Lady Bird, the nickname she had known almost all her life, or Claudia Alta, as she had been named by her parents.

She chose Lady Bird. "I long ago made peace with my nickname," she said. "At the age of thirteen I tried to get rid of Lady Bird once and for all. I entered a new school and promptly announced all around that my name was Claudia. But old friends infiltrated and the first thing I knew, there it was again." There have been many times since, when she would have preferred Claudia Alta—for instance, at a reception in the Governor's Palace in Jamaica, a year or so ago, she said, "Signing the guest book after Lady this and Lady that, I felt a little odd writing Lady Bird." But in the White House and to the millions who know her she wants to be Lady Bird.

It was a Negro nursemaid, Alice Tittle, who gave her the name when she was just an infant. She looked at the tiny brown-eyed baby girl and exclaimed, "Why, she's as purty as a lady bird," and that is what she has been called ever since.

Lady Bird had what many people would consider a lonely childhood but she has never viewed it that way. She was born and grew up in a very lovely old house in East Texas, near Karnack, called The Brick House because it was the only one for miles around made of bricks. The bricks, painted white, were made by slaves on the plantation before the Civil War, and it had been owned by a number of families before her father bought it some sixty years ago as the home for his Alabama bride.

All the fireplaces in the big house were blazing on that

cold dreary morning of December 22, 1912, when the country doctor, Benjamin Baldwin, brought Lady Bird into the world. Her two brothers, Thomas Jefferson Taylor III, eleven, and Antonio J. Taylor, eight, sensed that some important event was about to take place but they did not know what. They liked to spend the night with neighboring boys who lived some two miles away, and were always begging to go. That night they were granted permission without even asking. When they returned home the next day, they found they had a baby sister.

Lady Bird is of Spanish-Scottish ancestry on her mother's side, and English on her father's side. She is a Spanish-type beauty with black hair, sparkling brown eyes and flawless creamy-beige complexion. But the Scottish blood flows thick in her veins. Though her worth today runs into the millions, she is so thrifty that she insists on returning soda bottles promptly to reclaim the deposit, buys seconds in towels and household linens, and fills out her wardrobe at after-Christmas sales.

Her mother, the former Minnie Lee Patillo, descended from George Patillo, who came to America from Scotland in 1740. His sons settled in Georgia, after marrying wives in Virginia, and became prominent landowners. Some of them pushed westward to Alabama, where they became wealthy and were considered among the finest families in that state. Luther Patillo, Mrs. Johnson's grandfather, was born in 1842, and he married a widow, Sarah Jane Myrick Lewis. They had three children in addition to the beautiful, headstrong Minnie Lee, who eloped to Texas with Thomas Jefferson Taylor II. Luther and Sarah Jane Patillo's eldest son was Claude, born in 1872. He never married, was noted for his business ability, and was comparatively wealthy at the time of his death in 1941. (It was for him that Lady Bird was named Claudia.) Effie Mason Patillo was born in 1879, and she likewise did not marry. She had a strong influence on the early life of the present First Lady. Another son, Henry Gordon, born in 1882, died in childhood.

Lady Bird's father's family, of English extraction, were landholders in Alabama but they had not been too prosperous as farmers. At Evergreen, a community near Milton, young Tommy Taylor went to school with Minnie Lee Patillo, who was extremely pretty, intellectual and vivacious. Her schoolmates remember that she would bring wonderful tea cakes in her school lunch box and use them as bribes to get other students to do things for her. She was good at horseback riding, and on several occasions the Taylor farm was her destination, which, according to his half sister, Mrs. Harris H. Cory, thrilled young Tommy, who even then had a romantic interest in her.

In early manhood Tommy Taylor left his not too prosperous home and went to Texas where he established a business at Karnack, a raw frontier village of about a hundred people. Just over the Louisiana state line, it had been named after the temples of Egypt but some scholar had misspelled the name. After a few years Tommy Taylor returned to Alabama and married Minnie Lee Patillo against her father's wishes. He took her by train to The Brick House in Karnack. Here happiness was brief and intermittent for Miss Minnie, as everyone called her. She missed the refinements and culture she had known in Alabama. She was often lonely, for her husband was a successful businessman thanks to hard work as well as his business acumen. This left little time for the companionship and attention Miss Minnie missed. But as he prospered and expanded in business—his activities including farming, cattle raising, a store, a cotton gin, citrus-fruit growing and oil—Miss Minnie occupied herself at home with the largest library in the area. She had brought beautifully bound classics from her home in Alabama, and she encouraged the neighbors to use them. She also had a phonograph with stacks of records by Enrico Caruso and of various operas, which she played frequently for guests. Each year she went to Chicago for the opera season.

An intelligent woman with a strong sense of social justice, she was active in her own little projects to help the Negro tenants who worked on the farm. She was Red Cross chairman for that area of the county and often went out collecting things for that organization. She took a hand in politics, sometimes speaking out against a candidate who she felt lacked the qualifications for public office. In this, she was far ahead of her time, because at that time women had not even been granted the right to vote.

One of her closest friends was Nancy Lawrence, the teacher at the neighborhood Fern School the year before Lady Bird was old enough to enroll in the first grade. Minnie Lee Taylor and Nancy Lawrence shared a yearning for theater and music in this culturally barren frontier town, and several times they drove in Miss Minnie's car to Shreveport, Louisiana, forty miles away, to attend the theater or opera. On their return they would describe what they had seen and heard to the eager little Lady Bird. At Mrs. Taylor's suggestion, Miss Lawrence also prepared a preschool course for Lady Bird at the Fern School where her two brothers were already enrolled. Here, barely five years old, Lady Bird learned to read and to recite poetry. At recess, she would take walks in the woods with her teacher.

Lady Bird took her lunch to school, as did the other children. But because her father had a store, her lunch consisted of store-bought bread and luncheon meats. One day she noticed that a schoolmate's lunch consisted of a biscuit and a little jar of syrup. She watched him as he punched a hole in the biscuit and poured the syrup into it. She felt sorry for him and next day swapped her sandwiches for his biscuit and syrup, which she ate.

Although her father had 18,000 acres farmed by tenants, and was considerably wealthy when she was born,

Lady Bird did not live a life of luxury. She recalls that she read by an oil-burning lamp until she was nine years old—for electricity and gas had not yet come to that area—and she can easily remember the day indoor plumbing came to Karnack.

Lady Bird's first formal school days were spent in the one-room schoolhouse on top of a red clay hill. The number of her schoolmates—in grades ranging from one through seven—would vary depending on the tenant farmers in the neighborhood. Sometimes she would have as many as fourteen, and then, just before the school closed, a family with an abundant number of children would move away. Actually she finished one term when she was the only remaining pupil. But she has fond memories of those school days and likes to tell her daughters about them. "There was a big stove in the middle of the room, and it was always one of the big boys' job to bring in the wood and get the stove going in the morning. And then every Friday afternoon we had what they called exercises, which consisted of singing two or three patriotic songs. You learned them verse by verse, and I liked it. When I hear 'America, the Beautiful' or 'Columbia, the Gem of the Ocean' today, I know what the next lines are going to be because I remember them from the time I was six, seven or eight."

When Lady Bird was five years and nine months old her mother died. It was a tragic death but Lady Bird was not aware of it at the time. Her mother was walking up the circular stairway of the house when the family's collie ran under her feet, tripping her. She fell the full length of the stairs and was rushed to the hospital with painful head and spinal injuries. Subsequently she had a miscarriage and blood poisoning set in. On September 14, 1918, at the age of forty-four, she died. She never came home again and Lady Bird never saw her mother in death.

Lady Bird was aware her mother had gone away and sensed that everyone felt sorry for her, but she did not feel sorry for herself. "At five you are pretty insulated from pain, and besides that, I did not believe at the time that she was *gone.* I was quite sure she was going to come back . . . but as time went on, I quit thinking about it at all."

Even though they only had a few years together, her mother left a great influence on her life. She remembers her mother as a tall graceful woman with light-brown hair and blue eyes. She wore a lot of white and went around the house in a great rush—and she loved to read. "She would read to me," Lady Bird says, "and I remember so many things. All of the Greek and Roman myths and many of the German myths. Siegfried was the first person I was in love with."

After her mother's death, the neighbors stepped in to be substitute mother or big sister and to offer love, counsel and companionship to the little girl in the big brick house. One of these women was Mrs. Hugh Powell, who had lived in the big house herself as a little girl and now lives next door to it.

Despite this care from neighbors, T. J. Taylor disliked leaving his little daughter in the big house while he went off in the fall to his two stores and cotton gins. It was the busiest season of the year for him; he opened up early and stayed open until the last bale of cotton had been ginned, which was often one or two o'clock at night. Sometimes his older sons would be "shepherd" or "baby-sitter" to his little daughter, but by this time the boys were away in boarding school—Thomas Jefferson in New York, and Tony in New Mexico at the Los Alamos Ranch School. So Mr. Taylor began taking Lady Bird to work with him, letting her play around the store in the daytime, and at night she would sleep in a cot on the second floor of the store while he went about his business.

He was a man of very strong character; he was about six feet two, with very broad shoulders, and quite handsome. He lived by his own rules, which called for absolute honesty, but one night he told his little daughter a half-lie—"but a very sensible one," as she sees it now. He had tucked her in bed when she looked up and said, "Daddy, what are those long boxes?" They were coffins, but the little girl who had never seen death did not know. He hesitated a moment and then said, "Dry goods, honey." It was a long time before little Lady Bird learned the truth, but even at that early age she had heard ghost stories from her little Negro playmates and the housekeeper and such stories were very much a part of the lore of the countryside. To have known that she was sleeping on the second floor with coffins would have set her off and ended that arrangement promptly.

The summer when she was six her father sent her on the train—alone, with an identification tag around her neck—to visit her Aunt Effie in Alabama. She hadn't been there long, though, before Aunt Effie, a slight, sickly woman with dark hair and blue eyes, brought her back to Karnack and stayed there to take care of her. Those were happy days again for little Lady Bird. For Aunt Effie, a cultured woman, would read stories to her and thereby nurtured her love for literature, art and drama. As she grew older Lady Bird avidly read all the classics in her mother's library and was especially fond of Shakespeare. She also had a great love for nature. In the spring she, Aunt Effie and Dorris Powell would take long walks in the woods, hunting for the first violets, or take long drives to see the redbud and dogwood trees. In the autumn they would ride about, looking at the fall leaves, and try to decide which was their favorite season of the year. Mrs. Johnson still remembers those outings and wrote Mrs.

Powell recently from Washington that she wished she could return for a drive through the woods.

At night Lady Bird would watch for her daddy to come home from work, and she would run down the rutted road to meet him, asking what he had brought her that night. He often traveled the four miles from Karnack to The Brick House in a buggy drawn by a fine stallion, and raced it so fast that he could outdistance a car traveling the same route.

Lady Bird's playmates during those early years were the children of the Negro tenants on the farm and she thought nothing about the difference in their race. "I knew them better than anybody," she recalls.

A favorite outing was to Caddo Lake, a quiet, mysterious body of water shaded by age-old cypress trees draped with Spanish moss. As a little girl and later in her teens, she would go there with Aunt Effie, Dorris Powell and girlhood chums to fish, swim and picnic. One Saturday afternoon in the middle of May she went with Mrs. Powell and a group of high school friends from Marshall for a picnic. It seemed an ideal day for it—the leaves were already on the trees and the grass was green—but it soon started to get chilly. By noon it was so cold that they could not enjoy the lunch, so they drove back to Mrs. Powell's mother's house. By the time they arrived, snowflakes, a rarity in that section even in the winter, were falling and the girls had memorable fun running about the lawn catching snowflakes in their mouths during the thirty minutes or so the flurries lasted.

Mrs. Powell, who cut paper dolls for Lady Bird and sewed dresses for her dolls, recalls that the present First Lady was "a thinker" even as a little girl. "She was popular, pretty and an A-1 student, but she did not run with the herd. She was never identified with any group; she chose her friends because of their individual qualities, how they appealed to her."

Lady Bird was devoted to her Aunt Effie. "She opened my spirit to beauty, but she neglected to give me any insight into the practical matters a girl should know about . . . such as how to dress, or choose one's friends, or learning to dance." But Aunt Effie set the example for the generous humanitarian spirit Lady Bird has today.

During her first two years of high school, Lady Bird went to Jefferson, where she lived with Aunt Effie in an apartment, returning to The Brick House in Karnack on weekends. By this time Lady Bird was driving her own car, so when she became a junior in high school it was decided that she should live at home in Karnack and drive daily to Marshall High School in the county seat. Though she was only fourteen years old, she drove the fourteen miles of winding, unpaved road to and from school. This left her little time for social life with her classmates or extracurricular activities. When it rained and the roads became slick and muddy she would spend the night with friends in Marshall. On weekends she would bring two or three classmates from Marshall home to Karnack as her house guests.

One friend and classmate who has known Lady Bird since about the age of ten is Naomi Wheat (Mrs. William Bell of Marshall, Texas) and she remembers her as a quiet, dependable girl who was always neat and clean but did not give a hoot about fancy clothes. If Lady Bird was given a job to do, she was always there to do it. In her senior year in high school, Lady Bird was to be a princess in the May fete and had promised to help decorate the float that had to be ready by three on the afternoon of the parade. At four o'clock that morning, Lady Bird drove in from Karnack and was in Naomi's back yard in Marshall with her scissors to begin work on the float.

Looking back on her high school days, Lady Bird says

now that school must have been easier in those days than it is now, because she did not have any trouble making good grades. In the last month of school she began to realize that she was perilously close to having the best grades in class and it worried her greatly. It would mean that she would have to give the valedictory address and she was simply too shy to stand up and talk before an audience. She prayed that one of her friends, Emma Boehringer, would be the valedictorian and Maurine Cranson the salutatorian, and that she would come in third, because for that top honor she would not have to pay the price of making a speech. It turned out just as she prayed: Emma made a 95 average for the four years, Maurine had a 94.5 average, and Lady Bird had 94.

After graduating from Marshall High School in 1928, at the suggestion of Dorris Powell's mother, Lady Bird went to Dallas, where she enrolled in a junior college, St. Mary's Episcopal School for Girls. Aunt Effie went with her, but because she was in ill health she lived in a nearby nursing home. The greatest impact these two years had on Lady Bird's life was to enrich it spiritually. She had grown up a Methodist; at St. Mary's she went to the Episcopal church every day. She kept the prayer book at hand for frequent use. She found comfort and strength from the worship services for students. It was something she never forgot. After she left St. Mary's she felt that something was missing in her life. There was an emptiness she could not fill. After a few weeks at the University of Texas in Austin she decided it was the religious experiences she had enjoyed at the Episcopal school in Dallas that she missed. Soon thereafter she affiliated with the Episcopal Church in Austin and she has been a regular communicant of that faith ever since.

Going to the University of Texas was a big turning point in Lady Bird's life, but she almost did not go there.

After she graduated from junior college in Dallas, her Aunt Effie's health was failing and it became evident she could no longer follow and chaperone her young niece. It was proposed that she take Lady Bird back to Alabama to finish college when Gene Boehringer, who had become Lady Bird's best friend, heard about the plan and pleaded against it. She begged Mr. Taylor to send his daughter to the University of Texas, "since this is her home and her friends should be here."

As an inducement Gene invited Lady Bird to spend a few days in Austin with her to see if she liked the city and the university campus. "I fell in love with Austin the first moment I laid eyes on it, and it has never slackened since . . . it's a most wonderful town," Lady Bird declares.

For this, but not this alone, she will always be grateful to Eugenia Boehringer. Gene (now Mrs. E. H. Lassater of Henderson, Texas) was a native of Karnack and a sister of Emma Boehringer, who was valedictorian when Lady Bird graduated from high school.

"You know, there are some people who touch your life with something like a catalytic agent, bringing out qualities you might conceivably have and making them burgeon. Gene was such a person to me," Lady Bird says. "She was one of those tremendously outgoing people who made everyone around her feel a little more alive. You know, you kind of waited for her to come in. She always thought of interesting things to do, and I am a friendlier, more confident person today because of Gene." Gene also introduced her to people, advised her on how to dress, and above all "made me feel important for the first time."

Lady Bird loved the University of Texas and never wanted to leave Austin. Thomas Hagan, former head of the Washington bureau of the Miami *Daily News* and other Cox newspapers, and now a government official, sat in front of Lady Bird in one of her journalism classes. He remembers her as a very good student and one of the outstanding girls on the campus. He recalls that when the boys held a bull session in the fraternity house they always discussed the outstanding, most popular girls on the campus and Lady Bird was always among the ones named.

She got a Bachelor of Arts degree in 1933, graduating with honors in the top ten of her class. She had not decided what she wanted to do when she finished college but knew that she did not want to go back to Karnack to live. She got a second-grade teacher's certificate with the idea of trying to get a job in some faraway romantic spot like Hawaii or Alaska—"not in the town next door, because I did not have that much yearning to teach."

She also took typing and shorthand because she felt that once you got your foot in the door as a good secretary, if you had brains, personality and the desire to help, you could go just about anywhere in business. Then, because there was no great haste to get out of school, and it was not necessary for her to start making a living, and most of all simply because she adored the university, she stayed on for another year. This time she worked for a Bachelor's degree in journalism "because I thought that people in the press went more places and met more interesting people, and had more exciting things happen to them," she explains. She was on the staff of the campus daily. She was secretary to the student chapter of Theta Sigma Phi, the national honorary journalism fraternity for women, and on the executive council of the University of Texas Sports Association for intramural sports.

Lady Bird did not join a sorority, mainly because her father did not want her to. But she was popular and had what seemed like almost everything in those days: a beautiful new Buick when few college students even had a jalopy, a blank checkbook to spend money at will, and an open charge account at Neiman-Marcus in Dallas, a sophisticated status she had achieved, to the great envy of her friends, while she was still in junior college. "But," Dorris Powell recalls, "she used it wisely." She was prudent also in the use of her car and money.

"Bird was interested in books and the theater," says Mrs. Lassater, who was then working as secretary to C. V. Terrell, chairman of the Texas Railroad Commission in Austin. "She had a wonderful faculty for getting along with people. She never gossiped, and she was sincere in her conversation." She liked the new world Austin opened up to her, but she went back to Karnack during the summers between her college years. They were summers filled with leisure activity. She would travel back to Alabama to see kinfolks, and one year took a trip to Colorado.

To reward her for receiving her second degree from the university in 1934, Lady Bird's ever-indulgent father gave her a trip to Washington and New York. She was accompanied by her roommate. When Gene Lassater heard about the trip she exclaimed, "Oh, wonderful!" and gave them the name of a friend, Lyndon Johnson, to call upon in Washington. Lady Bird put the piece of paper on which Gene had written Lyndon Johnson's name in her purse. "But I did not call him and did not really ever intend to," she confessed recently. "For one reason, my roommate and I knew plenty of Texas-exes [as alumni of the University of Texas are called] in Washington and we were having a simply marvelous time sightseeing and being with them when we wanted to. Also, I would have felt odd calling up an absolute stranger."

Gene Lassater had met young Lyndon Johnson four years earlier when his father, also an employee of the Texas Railroad Commission, brought his son by and introduced him. Lyndon was teaching school in Houston then and was in Austin because his debate team was competing in the Texas Interscholastic League. After he went to Washington as secretary to Texas Congressman Richard Kleberg, he continued to drop by to see Gene when he was in Austin and she would arrange a date for him with one of the local girls.

Several weeks after her trip to Washington, Lady Bird was back in Texas and in Gene's office when in walked a young man—Lyndon. Her first impression of him was that he was "excessively thin but very, very good-looking with lots of hair, quite black and wavy, and the most outspoken, straightforward, determined young man I had ever met. I knew I had met something remarkable, but I didn't know quite what."

He asked the three of them—her, Gene and another friend, Dorothy McElroy, with whom he had a date that night—to go out with him and have a drink after work. It was then office closing time, so they did. Lyndon was obviously smitten by the young girl he had been hearing about. He asked her to join him for breakfast the next morning in the dining room of the Driskill Hotel.

"I was uncertain whether I wanted to or not, because I had a sort of queer moth-in-the-flame feeling about this remarkable young man," Lady Bird recalls. But since she was calling on her architect, who was going to remodel their house in Karnack—a project her father had promised she could supervise when she got home from the university —and his office was next door to the Driskill Hotel, she agreed to meet Lyndon.

On the way upstairs to see her architect she did not stop in the hotel, and Lyndon, who was eagerly waiting, did not think she would keep her date. But he continued waiting for her to come down. As she did, she looked in the window and saw him sitting alone. She went in and they had breakfast. Afterward they got into his car and drove into the country. "He told me all sorts of things that I thought were extraordinarily direct for a first conversation —his salary as secretary to a Congressman, about how much insurance he had, his ambitions, about all the members of his family. It was just as if he was ready to give me a picture of his life and of what he might be capable of doing."

Then he asked her to marry him. She did not say yes, and she did not say no. "I thought it was some kind of a joke," she recalls. But the next day he took her to meet his parents, and Lady Bird and Lyndon saw each other daily for four or five days after their first meeting. Another day he took her to meet his boss, Congressman Richard Kleberg, at the King Ranch. She found the Klebergs a most extraordinary family, living in a feudal domain, and Lyndon was very much the right hand of one of the brothers of the family.

Then the time came for Lyndon to return to his job in Washington, and he was planning to enroll in law school at night. She did not know when she would see him again and she longed to delay the parting although she was not yet ready to accept his proposal of marriage. So she suggested that since he had to drive through East Texas on his way back to Washington, they stop in Karnack so that he could meet her father. He agreed. He got a friend of his to drive his car, and he drove hers, and they started home.

Before she left Austin, however, she telephoned Dorris Powell with an urgent request: "Have The Brick House put in order and tell Isabel [the Taylor cook] to be ready to serve some guests. We are having visitors tonight." About dusk that evening she drove up with Lyndon, followed by his friend Malcolm Bardwell, secretary to another congressman. It was a pleasant, uneventful dinner as T. J. Taylor talked with and sized up his daughter's beau. And Lady Bird was sizing up her father's reaction. "I could tell that Daddy was right impressed with him," Lady Bird recalls. "After dinner he said in a quiet moment, 'Daughter, you've been bringing home a lot of boys. This time you've brought a man.' "

The next morning Mrs. Powell went to the Taylor house to meet Lady Bird's boy friend. Mrs. Powell reserved her judgment at first. She watched as Lady Bird walked with him to the crossroads when he left. They kissed before they parted. This was just too much for Dorris Powell. She stepped out into the road calling: "Don't do that! Hurry up, go on—or the Ku Klux Klan will get you." She urged the young man on his way before he completely swept her little friend off her feet.

Back in Washington, Lyndon enrolled at George Washington University night classes, and wrote or telephoned Lady Bird every day. He sent her a picture that touched her deeply. It was inscribed: "For Bird, a lovely girl with ideals, principles, intelligence and refinement from her sincere admirer." (On her fifty-first birthday last December 22, he gave her another picture of himself with the same inscription, only this time it said: "For Bird, *still* a lovely girl, etc.")

About seven weeks later, around the end of October, he returned once more to Texas and stopped overnight at the Taylor home. He began to be very insistent: "Let's go on and get married, not next year, after you've stayed home a year and spent time doing over the house, but about two weeks from now, a month from now, or right away." Lady Bird gave a rather indefinite yes. Together they went to Austin and picked out the ring at Carl Myer's. It was a modest diamond, and there was a wedding band to match it. But this they did not buy, Lady Bird says, because the wedding "was not firm enough at that time."

While Lyndon went on to Corpus Christi to take care of his boss's business, Lady Bird returned to Karnack, still not sure she was ready to take such an important step. She telephoned Dorris Powell in Marshall and asked her to come and spend the night. Lady Bird was wearing the diamond and they spent more than half the night talking about Lyndon, and whether she should marry him. "We begged her to wait six months," Dorris Powell recalls. But in the end Lady Bird decided to go to Shreveport, Louisiana, forty miles away, and buy her trousseau. Mrs. Powell went with her. They spent two days in Shreveport, bought lingerie, several dresses, and a three-piece suit ensemble in which Lady Bird was married. When they returned to Karnack, Lady Bird decided she just had to see Aunt Effie and tell her. Aunt Effie, with whom she had been living during the school semesters since she was six, spent most of the summer back in Alabama, and at that time was in a hospital there. "I wanted to tell her myself, for she had concentrated all her life and all her love on me, having no husband or children of her own, and I just knew that I had to go and see her," Lady Bird recalls.

She brought the picture Lyndon had autographed and sent her, and showed it to relatives in Alabama. One of them recalls that she laughingly said she was not sure she really liked the idea of wearing the name Johnson for the rest of her life. Just the same, it was obvious that she was in love with the young man.

It was a visit that added more to Lady Bird's indecision. She showed Aunt Effie the ring and told her she planned to marry Lyndon. Lady Bird says, "It was just as if I had stepped on a Cape jasmine or something—not only because I would be leaving her but because I would be taking the very hazardous step of marrying a stranger whom I had known less than two months. She was afraid for me and kept on repeating wise old adages like: 'If he loves you as much as he says he does, he will wait for you.' "

Lady Bird made no promises to Aunt Effie, just assured her that she loved her and that they would keep on seeing each other. When she got back to The Brick House in Karnack, Lyndon was waiting for her. She told him and her father what Aunt Effie had said. Her father, who always called her Lady, said, "Lady, if you wait until Aunt Effie is ready, you will never marry anyone." He told her to do what she thought was right, and added that he liked her young man. With just a little more such encouragement she could make a firm decision to marry. Her mind flashed again to her friend in Austin, Gene Lassater. "I'll go down and see Gene," she said, and packed her suitcase with her trousseau clothes. Lyndon went with her, and as they started he issued his ultimatum: "We either get married now or we never will. And if you say good-bye to me, it just proves to me that you just don't love me enough to dare to. And I just can't bear to go on and keep wondering if it will ever happen."

Lady Bird wondered if every prospective bride had to go through such indecisions. She was torn in two directions more deeply than ever. She did not want to let him go, but she also realized the hazards of the future. Only two days earlier she had read the marriage ceremony in her prayer book. "Do you realize what we are agreeing to?" she asked Lyndon. "I don't think he had ever read the marriage vows," she said later. But he persuaded her that then was the time for them to get married. At seven-thirty that morning he telephoned his friend Dan Quill, the postmaster in San Antonio, to make arrangements for the wedding to be held there that evening. So instead of going to Austin they headed for San Antonio, nearly four hundred miles away.

In the meantime Quill, an Episcopalian like Lady Bird, arranged to get the church and the minister, and also the marriage license. It was No. 104133, issued in the County of Bexar. The bride and groom were listed as Bird Taylor and Lyndon B. Johnson. The witnesses who signed the license, which was also a marriage certificate, were Cecille Harrison and Henry A. Hirshberg.

The ceremony was performed by the Reverend Arthur K. McKinstry, now retired bishop of the Episcopal Diocese of Delaware, then rector of St. Mark's Episcopal Church in San Antonio. At first he rebelled at performing the ceremony. He told Dan Quill: "You are asking me to perform a justice-of-the-peace ceremony. I don't marry people that fast. I want to get to know them, meet with them two or three days, talk with them and explain the seriousness of marriage."

But Postmaster Quill explained that Johnson had only one day in Texas, and the minister relented. Lyndon Johnson says now that he was still persuading Lady Bird to marry him as they walked up the church steps. It was to be a simple, quiet ceremony with no music and only two or three witnesses. In the church Lady Bird turned to her intended—the man who was to become known as the master of great detail—and asked, "You did bring a wedding ring, didn't you?"

The nervous bridegroom snapped his fingers. "I forgot!" While the rector waited, Dan Quill dashed across the street to the nearest store, a Sears, Roebuck, to get one. The clerk asked him what size. Quill, a bachelor, had not thought of that. So he took a whole tray of inexpensive rings back to church for the bride to select one that fit her finger. Quill paid $2.50 for the ring, his wedding gift to the bride and her husband, and it was used in the ceremony as they were pronounced man and wife. Later Lyndon and Lady Bird went to Austin and picked up the one that matched her diamond, and that is the one she wears. But she still has the other ring as a treasured keepsake.

As the young couple left the church, Reverend McKinstry remarked half to himself, "I hope that marriage lasts." The bridal party went to St. Anthony's Hotel, where they had a wedding supper. One member of the party rushed home and got a bottle of wine with which to toast the bride. Afterward Mr. and Mrs. Lyndon B. Johnson went to the Plaza Hotel where they spent the night. Before leaving for a Mexican honeymoon, they telephoned their family and friends the next day to tell them the news, and received their blessings. Dorris Powell ordered wedding announcements from J. A. Styron Engraving Company in Shreveport, Louisiana. The elegant script listed the bride as Claudia Alta (Lady Bird) Taylor so everyone would know who she was. Aunt Effie became reconciled to the wedding, and helped her in addressing the envelopes.

Reverend McKinstry sent the marriage license to the county clerk's office to be recorded. There was no address for either couple, so the clerk did not know where to return the document, which also serves as a wedding certificate. After recording it he pinned it to the sheet in the book. There it remained for more than twenty-five years. During this time Lady Bird and her husband often wondered what had happened to their marriage certificate, each thinking the other had mislaid it. Three or four years ago, Lyndon was to address a Rotary luncheon in San Antonio, and Quill, who had learned that their marriage license had never been returned, went to the clerk's office and claimed it. He telephoned Lady Bird at the ranch and asked her to come to San Antonio with her husband because he had a surprise for her—which, to her astonishment, turned out to be her long-lost wedding certificate.

[III]

The Man She Married

Lady Bird Johnson always calls her husband "Lyndon" when she is speaking about him. If she is speaking to him, she calls him "darling." Effervescent and affectionate, he will come home from his office and call, "Where's Mrs. Johnson? I want to kiss Mrs. Johnson." Then he asks for his children. He always thinks of her first in every crisis, every joy. Theirs is a happy relationship that is quite obvious to their children. Lynda Bird says, "Daddy worships Mother. He often likes to discuss some knotty problem with her and has great respect for her judgment."

President Johnson is not reticent about showing his love for his wife. He has an endearing way of kissing her on the forehead that bespeaks far better than words his feelings for her. When he took the oath of office as President in the giant *Air Force One* in Dallas on November 22, 1963, his first action was to turn and kiss his wife on the forehead. When he returned from a mission to Red-circled West Berlin for President Kennedy in the summer of 1961, she was in the White House rose garden along with President Kennedy and several other officials and news reporters. Mr. Johnson greeted her with a kiss. On their first visit to the glistening Taj Mahal in India, the marble tomb built by an ancient mogul for his beloved wife, Lyndon Johnson, then Vice-President, and Lady Bird sensed the significance of this beautiful monument to love. Under the brilliant noonday sun, he reverently leaned down and touched the top of her head with his lips. This romantic gesture was not lost on the natives or the guards on duty that day. One of the guards observed that it was the first time any visiting VIP had so responded to the spell of its splendor.

Lyndon Johnson is a husband who appreciates his wife and does not fail to let her and others know it. He says: "She's a wonderful woman. She has managed a radio business, the house, the kids and me—and you know, I guess I'm not the easiest person in the world to live with."

He sees her as a very shy, very selfless person, extremely perceptive, very durable and always thorough; generally prudent, gay and balanced. Her judgment on nearly everything, he says, is better than that of almost anybody he knows, except in regard to ladies' clothes. There, he thinks, she does not like things bright enough.

She is, he declares, what the analysts would call a perfect wife. She talks easily but never dominates the conversation; she is an avid reader who doesn't talk about books all the time; she is a businesswoman who makes her own money for several reasons: she plain likes making money, and she likes the independence that goes with it and the compassion that can be expressed with it. She never finds fault; if she disapproves, it is indicated by a certain aloofness and not by a catty remark. She genuinely seeks out the best in every person, and there is, her husband agrees, good to be found in everyone if you look for it.

He claims he has never heard her say a mean thing about anyone. He says that her workday is twice that of an ordinary person, but she never says she is tired. She has suggestions, solutions and ideas of her own for everything. She loves her own dear Southland but she is no "professional" southerner: you would never know she was from the South except for her accent. She is conservative and prudent when it comes to money, but she has a deep social conscience and is liberal in her views with respect to civil liberties and civil rights.

Those are the words and phrases her husband uses when he talks about her. He adds: "I am very proud of her. She is extremely helpful—she does her own job and a good deal of mine." What greater praise could a woman receive?

But Lady Bird Johnson's husband does not stop there. A man who always had great admiration and affection for his mother, he often compares his wife to her. He says: "I was one of five children, and I thought my mother was the greatest woman in the world. But I think Lady Bird spills out a great deal more of herself. Her children have a broader outlook because Lady Bird sees to it that they are concerned with everyone around them. She has prevented the spotlight from going to their heads and has taken care of them well.

"She is a combination of a very warm, understanding person who is patient and enduring and always genuinely just. I never saw her slice a corner on anything. She has great character. She is the first to tell me about any mistakes she has made—whether they are financial ventures or political boners—and to me that is a test of real character.

"She is the kind of person everyone in the world would want to be their trustee. I could not get five cents out of her I didn't deserve, and she wouldn't give me a penny less than I earned."

Only twice during the thirty years he has known her has he seen his wife really angry. Once was before they were married. They were on horseback to go riding; her horse backed up, he recalls, and she did not seem to know how to stop him. "I gave him a whack across the back. He leaped forward, almost unseating her, and she expressed herself to me pretty forcefully."

The other time her husband aroused her ire was when they finally found a house in Washington that they both wanted to buy, but Lyndon seemed to her to be endangering the purchase by offering the owner $2,000 less than was asked. That time she gave him a strong lecture: "I've lived out of a suitcase ever since we've been married," she said. "I have no home to look forward to, I have no children to look forward to, and I have nothing to look forward to but another election." Lyndon, chastened by her words, turned to his friend John Connally and asked, "John, what do you think I ought to do about that house?" Connally replied, "I would buy it," and Johnson did. He has never seen his wife angry since.

Lady Bird says there have been times when she has shown her anger, but each time afterward she "felt silly and absolutely weak. But," she adds, "it is probably not wise always to control one's temper. I think it might be better to blow up sometimes." But she wants to be "calm and reasonable and try to make those around me calm, help them to be."

"If she has one fault," her husband says, "it is that she just will not admit pain." She has lost four children by miscarriage, but she never complained or admitted her pain. Once he returned from a trip to Europe and found her ill in bed. But she assured him it was all right for him to go on to his office. Five minutes after he left she telephoned her doctor, who rushed her to the hospital and operated immediately. While talking to her husband she had been lying there in terrible pain with a tubular pregnancy.

Lady Bird Johnson has always recognized her husband's leadership. She says, "He is always prodding us to look better, learn more, work harder, and excel in all." She describes him as a "good man to have around in a crisis." She paid him the highest tribute a wife could pay a husband when she introduced him at a dinner a few years ago as "an exciting man to live with, an exhausting man to keep up with, a man who has worn well in the years we have been together, and, most important, a man from whom I've learned that to put all the brains and heart and skill you have into the job of trying to make your government work a little better can be wonderful life for a man and his wife."

An impetuous man, Lyndon Johnson has schooled Lady Bird over the years to expect the unexpected and to be unperturbed when he calls at the eleventh hour to say, "I'm bringing six guests for dinner." She has learned to keep the cupboard stocked with baked ham and smoked turkey to serve on short notice. Then, there have been times when she expected guests and had a lovely dinner waiting for them, only to have him call and say, "Come on down. We've decided to stay here and eat at the hotel instead." She never complains, but accepts these short-notice changes philosophically.

After they moved into the White House, he decided at noontime one day to give a reception at five o'clock for members of Congress who had not left Washington early to go home for Christmas. Some White House staffers threw up their hands when they heard it and said it could not be done—a reception for three hundred guests on four hours' notice. But Lady Bird and those who had worked for Lyndon Johnson longer knew it could be done. "You just move ahead and do the impossible," one of them says. "He likes 'can-do' people around him, and he expects you to do what he asks." The reception went off like a charm even if the last sprigs of holly were being hung as the first guests arrived and the newly lit fires in the fireplaces were still smoking.

Lady Bird never leaves her husband if she can help it, and is very much a part of the picture wherever he goes. Likewise, he wants her with him on every occasion possible. A few years ago he was on a speaking trip to North Carolina and decided in the early afternoon that she ought to be with him. He telephoned to Washington for her to join him. She was sitting under the dryer at the beauty shop when she got the message; she rushed home, dressed in her travel clothes, caught a plane, and was at his side three hours later shaking hands at a political rally.

Often when she gets invitations to be the honor guest at a women's party, or to make a speech where he is not invited, he shows up with her without warning, simply because he wants to be at her side and to help honor his First Lady. Needless to say, there is never a more welcomed uninvited guest.

"I want to ease the road, make it more comfortable and pleasant for Lyndon," says Lady Bird, "for if I leave any footprints on the sands of time, it will be because he has been able to achieve something." Her formula for keeping him healthy is to keep him happy.

Her husband is a man of strong self-discipline. For example, after he had a heart attack in 1955, the doctor limited his intake of calories to 1,500 a day. He set his limit at 1,200. When they wanted him to reduce from 200 to 180 pounds, he set his goal at 170. A former chain smoker, he tried only one cigarette after the attack, then kept a pack of cigarettes on his bedside table just to prove himself.

He is a man who prefers listening to reading; he gets most of his current knowledge from the spoken rather than the written word. But he never forgets a thing he hears—his memory is fantastic. He finds pleasure in things mechanical. At the LBJ Ranch, where he has had a loud-speaker installed and music piped into every room, he shows greater interest in the mechanism than the music.

He has a keen sense of humor and likes to joke with his family and friends. Some who do not know him so well take his jokes seriously. Lynda Bird once remarked, "The papers print Daddy's jokes as facts." His humor crops out in his off-the-cuff speeches, the kind he likes best. One of his favorite stories is about the southerner who claimed the South lost the Civil War because those "damyankees wouldn't fight with broomsticks." His response to extremely flattering introductions is to describe them as the "second best I've ever received. The first best happened back in the thirties when I went to a meeting in South Texas and the man who was supposed to introduce me didn't show up and I introduced myself."

Even during his hospitalization due to a heart attack, his humor came through. Lady Bird told him that the tailor who was making him two suits wanted to know what to do about them. He replied, "Tell him to go ahead with the blue one—we can use it no matter what happens."

When Lady Bird married Lyndon Johnson twenty-nine years ago she admitted she did not know everything about the dashing young man, but she loved him and wanted to share his life. Today, she is still not sure she knows all about him. Recently she remarked: "Lyndon is full of surprises. Take, for instance, his current project of collecting paintings from each of the countries we have visited."

She is proud to show this cultural facet of her husband's nature to their guests at the ranch, where the heterogeneous collection of paintings hangs in the President's study. From Italy there is a painting titled "The First Rain." "We appreciate that very much here where water means everything," Lady Bird remarks. There is a brightly colored painting from Jamaica with blue predominating, and from Greece a portrait of a "Wash Woman," and also an "Olive Harvest."

Despite the occasional surprises, Lady Bird has learned a lot about the President of the United States during their twenty-nine years together. She never tires of hearing him tell about his early life—the years before she met him. He was born on August 27, 1908, in a little three-room whitewashed farmhouse near Stonewall, Texas, where Sam Johnson, Jr., had brought his bride, Rebekah Baines Johnson, the year before. When his grandfather heard of the birth, he rushed from Johnson City, which he had founded as an Indian-fighting outpost fifty years earlier, to see his new grandson. "He's a fine child," he declared. "He'll be a United States senator some day."

Under the guiding hand of his mother, whom he describes as "a saintly woman," Lyndon developed fast. He learned his ABC's from blocks at the age of two, and at three he could recite *Mother Goose* rhymes and poems by Tennyson; at four he could read. When his mother read the Bible and ancient mythology to him, he showed an indication of what was to be a life-long passion for facts. "Is it true? Did it really happen?" he would ask.

For fear he would stroll down to the Pedernales River that flows nearby, fall in and drown when she was not looking, his mother sent him to the little white frame schoolhouse nearby when he was four. There he was the "baby" of the school. He sat in the teacher's lap as she taught him, and sometimes while she taught the other students. He never forgot that teacher, Miss Kate Loney, and she was one of his special guests at the 1961 inaugural in Washington.

When he was five his family moved to Johnson City, where he went to Blanco Elementary School and the Johnson City High School, from which he was graduated in 1926. The eager little boy who was impatient with his studies devised every scheme he could to evade study at home. But his mother was quick to catch on, and used her own tactics to make him learn.

Sometimes she would not find out until breakfast time that Lyndon was not prepared for a certain class; then she would get the book, place it on the table before his father, and the entire conversation between his parents was devoted to what Lyndon should have learned the night before. Lyndon was too well trained to interrupt the table talk and was forced to listen and learn. Many mornings his mother walked with him to the gate, asking him about his lessons to see that he was prepared for the day's work.

While he was still in grammar school Lyndon first announced his ambition to go to the United States Senate some day. It was during World War I and he was earning money shining shoes in the barber shop in Johnson City. His father had just taken over a newspaper (simply because the editor was ill and had been told by his doctor to go to Arizona) and turned the paper over to his mother to run. Lyndon had just started his shoeshine stand and was thinking of ways to expand his business—it was his own business and he was proud of it—when he heard a man deliver a lecture in which the theme was "it pays to advertise." Lyndon went to his mother and bought space on the front page of her newspaper to advertise his bootblack business. His father didn't know about it until the paper was off the press. He was so astounded that for years he told the story of his buying a paper so his wife could advertise that his son was a bootblack.

After graduating from high school, President Johnson

became what he calls a "school dropout." College was not in his plans and he organized a group of his friends into an expedition to California. They did not find fame or fortune in the West, however, and he returned, footsore, weary and hungry, to Johnson City to take a laboring job with a road gang, shoveling gravel and driving a truck. His main enjoyments in life were the Saturday night dances, and he would round up a truck full of young men in the neighborhood who paid fifty cents each for the ride into town to the dance.

One day his father told him, "A man who is satisfied to be a laborer will never have much on his mind. Of course there won't be much future in it, but those who are willing to devote all their lives to a road job really don't need much." This truth struck a responsive note in his son's fertile mind. Lyndon talked the matter over with his mother and the next day packed his clothes and started out for Southwest Texas State Teachers College in San Marcos. He borrowed $75 from the bank on his own note, and got a job, or a combination of jobs, to earn his way: school janitor and college secretary. As he did the sweeping he recited his lessons aloud; he practiced his oratory in the halls and made speeches to the walls; and he told tales of the heroes of history to the door mats.

He graduated after three years and later joined the faculty of Sam Houston High School in Houston where he taught public speaking and debate for two years. Politics was in his blood, and when the opportunity came to go to Washington as secretary to Representative Richard Kleberg, he did so with full family approval. There he was popular with other secretaries on Capitol Hill, and was elected Speaker of the "Little House," an organization of congressional secretaries.

A turning point came in his life soon after he married Lady Bird. After their Mexican honeymoon, they set up housekeeping in Washington in a modest one-bedroom apartment at 1910 Kalorama Road. This was a job for which Lady Bird was completely unprepared. "I had never swept a floor and I certainly had never cooked," she recalled. But she learned. She got a good cookbook and was soon preparing compliment-winning meals. Her talents showed up best, though, in the way she handled the family finances. Her husband's salary as a congressman's secretary was $267 a month. He took $100 out to make the payments on his car and insurance, and she ran the house with the remaining $167. From the very first she started buying what they called a "baby bond" each month. It cost $18.75, in ten years was redeemed for $25, and was to be saved for the day they started their family. Lady Bird found it easier to set aside the money for a person to come in once a week and scrub the bathroom and kitchen floors than to do it herself.

When they left Washington in July of that year, Lyndon returned to Texas as state administrator of the National Youth Administration. "If ever man met job, that was it," Lady Bird says. That kind of work was right down his alley, trying either to put young people back into schools if they could get them part-time jobs, or to teach them some skill. During those months their house in Austin was "a beehive—filled with folks who worked for the NYA or folks who needed jobs or folks who were just giving their advice on the NYA. It was the introduction to what the whole rest of my life has been like," she says in retrospect.

Then, in February, 1937, Congressman James Buchanan, an elderly man who was representing the Texas Tenth District, died. A seed that had long lain dormant in Lyndon Johnson's mind—that some day he would try for elective office—began to take sprout. With Buchanan's death, Lyndon talked to Lady Bird about it. He told her they must face one important fact—that he came from the smallest of the ten counties in the district, Blanco County, and that except for Austin he was virtually unknown in the other eight counties.

Actually, he was the least known of any of the ten people who entered the race, but Lyndon, who has a courageous, daring way of accepting every challenge, was the first to jump into the race. "I think his own decisiveness should get almost the entire credit for that," Lady Bird says, "although I went over to have a talk with that wonderful man State Senator Alvin Wirtz. He said it would cost about ten thousand dollars just to get in the race and make a good try for it, but I was ready to pitch in with anything I had in the way of financial help." She telephoned her father in Karnack and asked if he could get the ten thousand dollars for her as an advance against her inheritance from her mother's estate. He replied calmly, "Well, Lady, today's Sunday. I don't think I could do it before morning, about nine o'clock." The next morning he put it in the bank for her, and Lyndon and Lady Bird went to work.

Looking back on that first campaign, Lady Bird says, "Lyndon was never so young, never so vigorous, and never so wonderful! My only regret is that I did not have the gumption to share in it, although I suppose at that time I would have been looked upon as absolutely odd if I had gone around with him. In 1937, a wife didn't campaign." After he was elected they returned to Washington as Representative and Mrs. Lyndon B. Johnson.

He was assigned to the vitally important Naval Affairs Committee, and with the kindly guidance of his great friend Sam Rayburn, of President Roosevelt and of others in the Administration, he quickly established himself as a congressman who got things done.

He helped bring rural electrification to the vast farm areas of Texas; he fought for and won WPA funds to build the first of a series of lakes on the lower Colorado

River which have turned the Texas hill country between Austin and Johnson City into a lucrative resort area. One of those lakes (some of them were later built by the State of Texas) is named for his good friend and early political mentor, State Senator Alvin Wirtz.

With war clouds rising he also fought for enlargement and expansion of the naval base at Corpus Christi and many other improvements for that section of Texas. So well did he do his job in Washington that he was re-elected without even an opponent in 1938, 1940 and 1942.

Lyndon Johnson took his political gains gallantly, and he took his defeats the same way. The first came in 1941, and it was a hard one. For five days he thought he had been elected to the Senate in a race against former Texas Governor Willie Lee (Pappy) O'Daniel. Johnson had been announced the winner, three thousand congratulatory telegrams poured in, and he had practically hired a staff. Then, in a recount, the majority dwindled until on the fifth day he awoke to find that O'Daniel had the greater number of votes. He lost by 1,311 out of a million votes.

"A memory I will always have of him is the way he looked walking off to catch the plane to go back to Washington defeated," Lady Bird says. "I still see him walking toward that plane, looking very jolly and putting extra verve in his step, with his chin up. I think I know, too, just how much nerve and effort it took to keep up that appearance. But," she adds philosophically, "I think it was good for him. I can't say that a solid diet of success is good for anyone."

Lady Bird's life as a congressional wife was filled with activity—going with her popular young husband to social events for members of Congress, showing the Capitol and the rest of Washington to his constituents from Texas.

Her pilgrimages to Mount Vernon were innumerable. She kept a record of them for years, until she got way past two hundred and just stopped counting. She took one group down to the first President's home in a snowstorm, and they arrived so late that the gates were closed. But because she was a congressman's wife and the guards recognized her from her many visits, they let them inside and even permitted them to go into rooms on the third floor normally closed to visitors.

Lady Bird's interest in shepherding his constituents around Washington pleased Lyndon because it meant she would not be lonely while he spent long hours on his job. It also kept her in touch with what he was doing and the people for whom he was working.

In the late summer of 1941, the House was wrangling over a Roosevelt Administration measure to extend the Selective Service Act by permitting the continued drafting of young men for military training as a preparatory move in the event the threatening war clouds on the horizon should burst. Lyndon Johnson was one of Sam Rayburn's floor men who tried to get every member of the House to come and vote and to sell them on why to vote for the extension. Lyndon Johnson did his job well. He told his colleagues that if war came, he himself would volunteer for active duty. It was then just three months before Pearl Harbor and the measure passed by one vote.

Not long ago Lady Bird asked her husband what three pieces of legislation he was proudest of having had a hand in during his twenty-three years in Congress. This extension of the draft when danger was so imminent was the first one he named. Then, in rapid order, he named the Civil Rights Act of 1957, which was the first such legislation in eighty years, and the third was the Space Act, which opened the way for further U.S. advances in space exploration.

. . .

On December 8, 1941, when Congress declared war, Lyndon Baines Johnson kept his promise. He was in the naval reserve and he asked for active duty. He got it. "The question was, what would I do?" Lady Bird recalls. "I decided to go to work in his office and keep the line of contact with three hundred thousand people in the Tenth District of Texas." And she was a volunteer in the best sense of the word. She worked without pay. "That experience," she has said, "was the best thing that ever happened to me, because after about three or four months I felt for the first time that if it were necessary, I could make my own living—and that is a good feeling to have. But best of all, it gave me a greater understanding of Lyndon.

"By the time the end of the day came, when I had shifted my mental gears so many times—from talking to the mayor of Austin about the new abattoir that they just had to build and materials were scarce (you had to get a permit from the government to use steel and such), and next talking to somebody on the telephone who wanted a government priority for something else—I was utterly exhausted. I didn't even want to make an unimportant decision. I wanted one of my good friends to tell me where we would eat, what we were going to have—to spend a pleasant two or three hours, that was all." From this experience, too, she came to understand what had sometimes seemed to her Lyndon's unwarranted irritations when he did that job.

She rented out their house for $100 a month and went to live in Virginia in a $60-a-month apartment with Nellie Connally, wife of the present Governor of Texas, who was then on duty in the Navy. Nellie was also working in her husband's place in Johnson's office.

Sharing these wartime experiences and months of waiting, the days of anxiety when Lyndon was gravely ill in the Far East, and again when he narrowly escaped death as his plane crashed in Australia, Lady Bird and Nellie became as close as sisters. In August, 1942, Lyndon came back to his seat in Congress, wearing the Silver Star that General Douglas MacArthur had awarded him in the Pacific. But he did not come back of his own choosing. President Roosevelt had summoned all members of Congress to return to their first duty to their country.

In 1948, Lyndon felt it was time to run for the Senate again. He received encouragement from friends in Texas and Washington including President Truman, and he announced his candidacy from his steps of the White House. It turned out to be a sort of endurance contest.

In the first primary, Lady Bird and Lyndon put everything they could into the race, and were dreadfully disappointed when he came out almost hopelessly behind. But Lady Bird had just begun to fight. With her encouragement they decided to pick up and try real hard again in the second primary. For the first time she really campaigned. When the ballots were counted it was agonizing. Dozens of boxes were contested all over the state. In the end Lyndon won by eighty-seven votes, and when they returned to Washington he was welcomed in the Senate with a new nickname, "Landslide Lyndon."

In the Senate, Lyndon worked even harder than in the House. He quickly rose to the top and in 1955 was elected majority leader. That was a coveted honor, but it meant more work and there were, after all, only twenty-four hours a day in which to do it. Sometimes he seemed to work all twenty-four. Lady Bird did what she could to give him an oasis of peace and rest at home but it was impossible to slow him down. He was determined to put his legislative program through.

On Saturday, July 2, Majority Leader Lyndon Johnson was back at work on Capitol Hill at his usual whirlwind pace. He breezed through half a dozen conferences, rushed downtown to have a tailor fit a new suit, returned to luncheon and a checkup by the Capitol physician, who found him fit, and a press conference at which a reporter's persistent questions irritated him. By late afternoon he was en route to Middleburg, Virginia, to spend the week-end at the estate of George Brown, a Texan. But he began to feel a tightness in the chest. He was ashen when he arrived at the country estate, and did not join the other guests, many of them senators, at the swimming pool. Against Lyndon's wishes, Brown called a local physician, who ordered Johnson rushed to Bethesda Naval Hospital. Lady Bird was notified at home of his illness, and went to the hospital to await his arrival.

When he learned what was the matter with him Johnson did not panic. He calmly asked his doctor for three minutes to see three people: Felton Johnson, secretary of the Senate; George Reedy, his executive assistant; and Lady Bird.

He told Felton Johnson to call Senator Earle Clements, who was back in Kentucky campaigning, and tell him to carry on as majority leader, since, if he survived, he would not be back that session and did not want any question to arise as to the leadership of the Senate. He asked Reedy to call the news services and tell them he had had a heart attack, moderately severe. "Don't tell them I'm here for a rest or a checkup," he said. To Lady Bird he said, "Honey, here is my money clip; you may need some. I think we're going to lick this thing. My will is down in your general manager's desk at Austin [where Lady Bird owned the radio and television station]. Do one thing for me—get me the best heart specialist." Then he said to his doctor, "I'm ready for you." Later that evening Lyndon Johnson went into shock and for the rest of the night his life hung precariously in the balance. He was in an oxygen tent. Lady Bird moved into the hospital in an adjoining room.

Gradually he began to rally, but he was in the hospital for five weeks.

Letters of cheer, good wishes and prayers for his recovery poured in from all over the country, from people in all walks of life—United Auto Workers' President Walter P. Reuther; CIO-AFL Secretary James Carey; RCA Head David Sarnoff; former Senator Tom Connally; Elder Statesman Bernard Baruch, who penned a note to his typed letter saying, "Preserve your strength, we are going through trying times and no one will be needed more than you." From President Eisenhower was a letter he never signed because he himself suffered a heart attack after dictating the letter; Senator John F. Kennedy scrawled a personal note saying that "all the Kennedys are praying for you"; Cowboy Star Gene Autry, who had campaigned with Lyndon in his 1948 race for the Senate, wired, "Get back in the saddle again real soon"; Virginia Senator Harry F. Byrd wrote Lady Bird, "Give Lyndon my best; tell him the Senate is not the same without him"; Arizona Senator Barry Goldwater wrote, "It is difficult to understand that a heart as big and as strong as those bred in Texas can ever have anything wrong with it, but I suppose it can happen even to people from the Lone Star State . . . Please take care of yourself and do what the doctor tells you to do because we can't take chances with Americans like you."

But perhaps Senator Hubert H. Humphrey summed up things best in his letter. He wrote: "The Senate just isn't the same without you. I miss having you get after me; I miss your good humor. Yes, we're just lonesome for you. We hear good reports on you. I gather you are getting more and more opportunities to read and rest and think than ever before in your life. Once you recover, God only knows what will happen around this town. Lyndon Johnson tired was a fireball. Lyndon Johnson rested will make the atom bomb obsolete. Lyndon Johnson harassed and busy had more ideas in one day than Solomon had in a week. Imagine Lyndon Johnson calm, rested and intellectually primed. I don't know, maybe I ought to resign and get out of here before you return. I'm getting old. I had a tough time keeping up with you before you went to the hospital. It will be impossible when you return to the Senate."

"I understand," Adlai Stevenson wrote Lady Bird after her husband began to mend, "that Lyndon is being a juvenile delinquent in the sick room. If he doesn't behave, let me know and I'll bring a posse of assorted Democrats to bring him into line."

While Lyndon Johnson argued with doctors and nurses to let him see his staff and take care of things from his bed, Lady Bird stayed at his side. She recalls: "Lyndon wanted me around him twenty-four hours a day. He wanted me to laugh a lot, and always to wear lipstick. During those days we rediscovered the meaning and freshness of life."

She converted her hospital room into an office and tried to answer as many of the letters as possible. It was in effect a training in handling the avalanche of mail she receives today as First Lady, mail which she insists on reading and answering herself. Many of the people to whom she replied when her husband was ill wrote again because her letters were so personal and friendly. Lady Bird saved dozens of letters, typical of the thousands received, and put them between acetate sheets in gold-tooled leather scrapbooks that are now on the bookshelves in the family sitting room at the White House. They are souvenirs of the great outpouring of love, friendship and concern for a man who was serving his country well.

On August 14, Lady Bird took her husband back to their ranch in Texas. He looked thin and pale in comparison to his old self. His clothes hung loosely on his slim lean frame as they walked down the ramp from the plane to greet the Texans turned out to welcome him back to the country where, he says, "they know when you're sick, care when you die, and love you while you live."

Both Lady Bird and Lyndon looked back on the dark days of anxiety and pain to find something good in their experience. "You realize how many wonderful people there are in the world," Lyndon said. "I got reacquainted with my family. Lady Bird says she loves me better than ever. Everybody loves Lyndon, I found out."

"It was a rugged experience, full of worry and requiring patience, but it opened new vistas, some of which have paid dividends," Lady Bird says. There were the letters—"sweet, thoughtful, kind letters"—that arrived while he was in the hospital, and then, when he was ready to go home, someone broadcast that she needed recipes for tasty dishes with low-fat and low-calorie content called for in the rigid diet his doctors insisted he must stick to if he expected to get well. More letters poured in. "Some of the recipes have proved quite helpful; some people sent in their grandmothers' tried-and-true recipes; some sent new scientific booklets. I'm either going to have to turn registered chemist, though, or jump out the window," she added with a laugh.

Lady Bird had come through another crisis smiling.

There was another family crisis to face after he became Vice-President. Already, with two teen-age daughters in the family, the white brick house they had bought before World War II was bursting at the seams, and all felt it was time to make a move in Washington. The big question was, where? They had trouble finding a place that met their needs at a price they were willing to pay.

It had been suggested that they move into a hotel inasmuch as all their public duties were multiplied by Johnson's position as Vice-President, but Lady Bird held out for a house. Finally, in his impulsive manner, the Vice-President made a move on his own. He had gone with Mrs. Johnson and his daughters to a Mardi Gras Ball in the Sheraton Park Hotel, which has an entire wing of hotel apartments. He saw Barbara Norton, the hotel's public relations director, who had been urging him to move into the hotel, and an idea flashed into his mind. "Barbara, where's the manager? I want to look at one of the apartments," he told her. Quickly Barbara located the manager and the three walked to the east wing. He was shown a suite of eight spacious rooms, luxuriously furnished: four bedrooms, living room, dining room, den or library, kitchen and five baths. "I like it," he declared. "All I've got to do is sell Lady Bird. I used to sell hosiery door-to-door and if I can sell hose, I can sell Lady Bird on this." A few days later he signed the lease. They lived in the hotel for six months.

In the meantime Lady Bird had found the house she wanted. It was Perle Mesta's beautiful French château on a hilltop in Washington's exclusive Spring Valley section. Negotiations were under way when the Johnsons left for their trip to Southeast Asia in April, 1961, and the transaction was completed while they were gone.

Mrs. Mesta's house turned out to be Mrs. Johnson's dream house. The details and appointments Mrs. Mesta had added were elegant and beautiful. The damask on the walls of the drawing room was from a French château; the parquet floors in the library, the dining room and the drawing room had been taken from a château and shipped over in sections approximately three feet square; the paneling in the library was also from a château, in Versailles. The murals on the dining-room wall were Viennese, dating back a hundred and fifty to two hundred years, and the lights were old Waterford crystal chandeliers. Much of the furniture, which was purchased with the house by the Johnsons, had been copied from pieces

Mrs. Mesta had seen in France, and the handsome iron gates at the entrance came from a Long Island estate.

Mrs. Johnson added her own touches to stamp it with the LBJ personality. When she moved to the White House last December, she went through the emotional experience of dismantling and deciding what to do with her treasures at The Elms. As she looked lovingly at each piece that had made up her dream house, she would sigh and say, "I'll never have a home this elegant again." But because of her frugal nature, she could not bring herself to keep the house and not live in it. And the President, thrifty in his own way (he goes around turning off lights to save electricity), concurred.

[IV]

Life in Washington

People sometimes get the idea that life in Washington is a gay round of cocktail parties and receptions at which the same people—those who run the government and those who want to influence them—show up night after night at the same places to brush elbows, pick brains and push pet projects. It has not been that way for Lyndon and Lady Bird Johnson during most of the twenty-six years they have been in public life in the nation's capital.

"Lyndon isn't the darling of Washington social life," Lady Bird told Texas friends several years ago. "He can accept very few invitations, not because he is unfriendly but simply because there is not time. He always says that every job he has is bigger than he is, that he has to work twice as hard as the next man to do it right, and what that means is that he is usually working at the Capitol until eight, nine or ten o'clock every evening. We can very seldom go to cocktail parties because they run between five and seven-thirty. Likewise, we can accept few invitations that involve white tie and tails or even a dinner jacket. It just takes too long to drive all the way home to change and start out again.

"What he likes best in the way of entertaining," she continued, "is to have Texas friends out to dinner and talk about Texas, or to take such close friends as Speaker Sam Rayburn, Senator Dick Russell [of Georgia], or Senator Stuart Symington [of Missouri] out for a quiet dinner and lengthy discussion of plans and programs for future work in the Senate."

This changed when he became Vice-President, as did her own daily schedule. As Vice-President, he did not have to remain on Capitol Hill to thrash out the problems of the sometimes unwieldy Senate long after darkness had settled over the city and the government workers had returned to their suburban homes in nearby Maryland and Virginia. Now that was someone else's job. He had other duties, and while they were important, they were not so arduous. Since the President himself could not go out and mingle and talk with people to learn of their thinking and temper, his Vice-President did. He was eager to know what people from all walks of life—government, labor, business, Congress, embassy row and the nation's press in Washington—were thinking and talking about—and doing.

This brought about many changes in Lady Bird's life. For one thing, it meant meeting many new people; it also meant a bigger wardrobe, because as wife of the Vice-President she could not show up night after night in the same cocktail or evening dress. And she had to plan her own daily activities to be available to accompany her husband on his schedule.

A few months before she became First Lady, a reporter asked her what she did as wife of the Vice-President. She whipped out her date book and ran through her schedule of the previous day. It ran like this:

> 9 A.M.—Spanish lesson, interrupted to make appointment for Lynda with the dentist and for Lucy with a geometry tutor.
>
> 11 A.M.—Opened the National Cathedral Flower Show.
>
> 1 P.M.—Attended luncheon for the Heart Fund Drive with "appropriate remarks" in hand.
>
> 2:30-5 P.M.—Dictated mail, paid bills and signed KTBC [radio and TV station owned by Mrs. Johnson] checks, with time out to find my last hat in the attic for a church bazaar.
>
> 5 P.M.—Entertained 35 students en route to Chile with the Peace Corps.
>
> Emergency call sent me dispatching Lyndon's tux (with all studs, I hoped) to the Capitol.
>
> Dressed and joined him at 7:35 in front of the White House for dinner that night.

At the conclusion, the reporter said, "I know, Mrs. Johnson, but what do you really do?"

"Actually the question is one that every woman, and especially every wife involved in public duties, frequently asks herself," Mrs. Johnson says today. "Anne Lindbergh called it 'fragmentation of self.' You just hope that all your efforts add up to something worthwhile." Every mail brought requests for her to serve as patroness or sponsor of some charitable or educational benefit. Finally the requests became so numerous—and many of them from people who had also solicited Mrs. Kennedy, the First Lady, to be a patroness—that something had to be done. Mrs. Kennedy worked out an arrangement with Mrs. Johnson whereby they did not both lend their name to the same benefit the same year. Even so, both were kept busy.

Mrs. Johnson's first official act as Second Lady was to launch a ship at the Bethlehem Steel Company's Shipbuilding Division at Sparrows Point, Maryland, four days after the inauguration. Vice-President Johnson and a host of friends from Texas in Washington for the inauguration accompanied her by train to Baltimore where she swung the champagne bottle on the bow of the ship in ten-degree weather. Her matron of honor at launching the large ocean-going merchant vessel, owned by the Lykes Brothers Steamship Company of New Orleans and named the S.S. *Solon Turman* for its president, was Nellie Connally, whose husband was President Kennedy's nominee for Secretary of the Navy.

This was followed by many citations to accept, luncheons and balls to attend. In October, 1961, she was given a crystal vase citation from the Fashion Group of Philadelphia for her "example and influence on women in public life" and went to Philadelphia to receive it at a glamorous charity ball. She wore her inaugural ball gown of Persian-coral coupe de velour. After a tour of the Philadelphia Museum of Art, she danced with Philadelphia Mayor Richardson Dilworth, and stayed on for the fashion show and champagne supper afterward. Near midnight, she returned to Washington with her press secretary, Elizabeth Carpenter.

At a Valentine's Day luncheon she received the Washington Heart Association's Distinguished Achievement Award in recognition of her "years of friendship with the Heart Association . . . the time she gave to the heart cause . . . and finally for her example in facing cardivascular illness in her own family." The Washington Hebrew Congregation presented her with a silver loving cup in recognition of her talents as "mother, wife, homemaker and a leader among women." She was cited as a "good-will ambassador of the world" by the National Association of Colored Women's Clubs at their 1963

Washington convention, and received the Humanitarian Award from the Ararat Chapter of B'nai B'rith in Hartford, Connecticut, for her "understanding heart and dedication to humanity."

She was the first woman to receive the Volunteers of America's "humanitarian citation" and she went to Cleveland to accept that. In Austin, the Federation of Business and Professional Women's Clubs of Austin gave her its annual Business Woman's Award. She served as sponsor of the Wellsley Club Woodley Dancing Class in Washington and the annual Azalea Festival in Norfolk; as patroness of the Woman's National Democratic Club's fund-raising all-states bazaar, the Hexagon Club's benefit show for Children's Hospital, Congressional Circle for Friendship (neighborhood) House; and as honorary chairman of the Independence Ball sponsored by the State of Israel Bonds in Washington to celebrate Israel's fifteenth anniversary.

It was for this sponsorship that she received the sharpest public criticism in her life. An Arab diplomat, Najdat F. Safwat, chargé d'affaires at the embassy of Iraq, sent her a letter, which he made public, asking her "in the name of Arab-American friendship to consider the feelings of the one hundred million Arabs when they hear of your support and role in the Israel Independence Ball" to withdraw her name and support.

She replied to the diplomat: "The easiest course for the wife of a public official would be, of course, never to lend name, hand or heart to any endeavor, charitable or commemorative. Alas, letters such as yours make this procedure even more tempting.

"However, I have, for whatever small value it may be, tried to be accessible and available to as many as possible without distinction as to religion, race or region, and certainly including all states of the Near East. I shall continue to do so."

Several senators took the floor to protest such criticism of the Second Lady by a foreign diplomat, and a flood of mail poured in at The Elms supporting her stand and praising her for maintaining it.

Shortly after her husband became Vice-President, Mrs. Johnson formed a small class to learn Spanish. Four close friends met in her home three times a week for two hours of study under the tutelage of Guatemala-born Elsa McGuire. Her four classmates were Mrs. William O. Douglas, wife of the Associate Justice of the Supreme Court; Mrs. Thomas Dodd, wife of the Connecticut senator; Mrs. Frank Church, wife of the Idaho senator; and Mrs. William White, wife of the syndicated columnist. When she was away on travels in this country and abroad, Mrs. Johnson took her Spanish book along to keep up with the class.

"Sometimes she would come in exhausted to Spanish class," Mrs. Church recalls. "But she felt that this hemisphere is terribly important and wanted to be able to speak the language of the people who live in it. She felt also she was doing it for her own mind, and anything she does to improve herself pleases her."

Sometimes the class would be interrupted by the Vice-President, who would rush in from another room where he was working and ask, "Bird, where's this?" or "Where's that?" and she knew personally where everything was. "It made all of us feel at home because that was just the way our husbands are at home," one of the students said.

A couple of years earlier she set out to learn Russian, something her husband boasted about at a Senate appropriations subcommittee hearing when it received a report on the growing number of foreign service officers taking foreign-language training. It was proof that although, in her words, he "constantly prods" her to continue self-improvement, he is proud of her every accomplishment.

Lady Bird Johnson's life in Washington during those busy days as Second Lady were studded with quick-flying trips to various points of the globe: on missions with her husband abroad, on his speaking and political trips around the country, and on her own speaking trips. Once she traveled to West Virginia to break ground in pouring rain for a new community library at St. Albans, carrying along an armful of books autographed and donated by VIP's. There was an autographed copy of President Kennedy's *Profiles in Courage*, and three books inscribed by Mrs. Kennedy: *A Tour of the White House with Mrs. John F. Kennedy*, *Masterpieces of Painting at the National Gallery of Art*, and a copy of the official White House guidebook. Vice-President Johnson autographed *Citadel*, the story of the United States Senate by his long-time friend William S. White, and Mrs. Johnson inscribed *The Living Jefferson*, her favorite biography of Thomas Jefferson. She carried also a copy of *Daniel Boone: Opening to the Wilderness*, autographed by her two daughters, and several books authored and autographed by Juan Bosch, then President of the Dominican Republic.

Mrs. Johnson had returned just the day before from the Dominican Republic, where her husband had been President Kennedy's representative at the inauguration of President Bosch. He sent his biography of the biblical king, *David*, and a collection of short stories he had written in exile. His inscription on each was: "To the students of West Virginia with best salutations by order of Mrs. Lyndon B. Johnson, agreeably obeyed by Juan Bosch."

Following the library ceremonies, Mrs. Johnson went

on to Charleston, West Virginia, to inspect the Area Redevelopment Agency's job retraining program at the Charleston Memorial Hospital. Before returning to Washington from West Virginia that day, she gave a political talk also at a state-wide Democratic women's conference.

"White House dinners have always been a choice invitation and Mrs. Kennedy made them especially so," Mrs. Johnson said a few months before she became official hostess at the White House. "I can remember the long line in the old days at the annual congressional receptions where the members of Congress waited to shake hands with the President and First Lady—the husband always looking a little miffed for he had been cajoled into white tie and tails, and the wife looking very pleased in her beautiful ball gown. With ease and grace Mrs. Kennedy has removed much of the stiffness, eliminated the long receiving line and made the White House a showcase for great artists, writers and other intellectuals of this nation."

Dinner guests at the White House during the Kennedy Administration were frequently seated at tables of ten and twelve instead of at the long horseshoe table of previous years. This made it possible to converse with several persons instead of just the gentleman on either side, a practice Lady Bird is following herself as White House hostess.

In between her official and social responsibilities, Mrs. Johnson, as a senator's wife and as Second Lady, had a number of domestic duties to perform that wives and mothers throughout the country do for their husbands and children, and she still has. She looks after the little details of everyday life: lays out his suit each morning and has his fountain pens filled with ink and placed in the right pockets; sends his clothes to the cleaner's and sees that each suit is back in time for the occasion he wants to wear it; lets him get away with keeping late hours, but sees that he doesn't skip meals or eat forbidden desserts.

When he was the top Democrat in the Senate she often telephoned him around six-thirty or seven at night and started to drop hints—not subtle but humorous—about wanting to be taken out to dinner. Usually he gave in by eight o'clock. "If I had left him alone, he wouldn't have eaten until midnight," she says. In the White House she worries about his long hours and rapid pace without rest. One day in early January she pinned a note to his pillow suggesting he rest for an hour and a half in the middle of the day. "It was a recommendation that sounded more like a doctor's order," the President said.

One of her biggest problems in Washington as wife of the Vice-President was getting away from people, parties and telephones to a quiet oasis. One day she was at home preparing a speech for delivery before the American Women in Radio and Television in New York and for that sophisticated national audience she wanted to have an especially challenging message. She was interrupted every few minutes by the telephone, the electrician, or painters wanting to know where something should be placed in the house they had recently purchased from Perle Mesta.

To escape the interruptions Lady Bird got into her car, bringing her "speech pad," drove to a drive-in restaurant and ordered something to eat. While she munched a sandwich, she finished writing her speech. It was well received, and the challenge struck a responsive note. Even President Kennedy commended her on it when he saw her the following night at a White House dinner.

She told the woman broadcasters: "You have in your hands the media with which to wipe out generations of illiteracy. The village woman in Southeast Asia may never learn to write, but she can see and hear. With her neighbors she could learn the rudiments of good health, the way to scrub the vegetables, the way to care for the baby. Countries which might never hope to afford thousands of books to teach their people to read and write can afford one book to show on television. The quickest answer to those three words—poverty, disease and illiteracy—may lie in our very own media and may lie in your very hands."

One of Lady Bird Johnson's greatest pleasures as a congressman's wife was showing friends and constituents around Washington. "There are few things I enjoy so much as being a guide on a tour. Maybe it is because I still like all the sights myself, and you get a variety of visitors. The school children want to see the original Star-Spangled Banner, or the plane in which Lindbergh flew the Atlantic; the art lovers want to see the latest exhibits at the Corcoran or the National Gallery of Art. Many ladies want to see the home of Washington hostesses such as Perle Mesta and Gwen Cafritz. Then, of course, most everybody wants to see the Capitol itself, to hear the Senate and House debate and see the statesmen whose names are household words.

"I particularly enjoy a visitor who wants to go to a committee hearing. That's where the legislation is really thrashed out, where the good and the bad are decided during the debate." She recalled one day years ago attending a Senate committee hearing on whether to send troops to Europe just after the end of World War II. "We heard the views of such men as Herbert Hoover, Thomas Dewey and Robert A. Taft that day and it was a thrill to listen to the different viewpoints of those great public leaders. We were seeing history made right before our eyes, and I treasure such memories."

Although she still clings to the friends she had during her early years as a congressional wife, many of them also wives of congressmen, Lady Bird somehow finds time for the legions of new friends she has met in her expanding role as Second Lady and now First Lady. She has always been extremely popular with wives of members of the Senate and treats them all with the same degree of friendliness. However, she is particularly close to Rosemary Smathers, wife of Florida Senator George Smathers; Bethine Church, wife of Idaho Senator Frank Church; and Abigail McCarthy, wife of Minnesota Senator Eugene McCarthy.

One Senate wife who has known her for six or seven years describes the new First Lady as "a warm person who always greets you with a gay smile and both hands outstretched. Her real interest is in everything she does. It is surprising how easy it is to talk to her and how much she understands your problems. She really sets an example for congressional wives—you see how much she helps her husband and yet takes care of her home, her children and her business and you think you can do it too.

"And one very rare thing," this Senate wife added. "I don't remember her ever saying an unkind word about another woman or about life in Washington. She doesn't gossip; she's too busy looking for the best in everyone to poke into other people's dirty laundry."

She added an opinion as to why Lady Bird is able to crowd so much activity into one day, or one week: "She has no façade; she is doing the thing she is interested in, and she is used to running her business, running her life and making speeches."

One of Lady Bird's close, old-time friends is Perle Mesta, former United States minister to Luxembourg, Washington party-giver and friend of VIP's. When Lyndon Johnson did not get the presidential nomination in 1960, Perle, who had given a lavish party for him during the Democratic National Convention, found this defeat of her favorite political friend hard to accept. At a party she gave during the 1956 Democratic Convention, Perle introduced him as her candidate for President, but then he had responded with, "Quit your kidding, Perle." During the 1960 campaign, Perle was conspicuously silent, but she was still Lyndon and Lady Bird Johnson's friend. After she sold her elegant Normandy-style mansion to the new Vice-President as a residence befitting his new position, she moved into a skyscraper apartment where she gave a party to celebrate Lady Bird's fiftieth birthday. Knowing Mrs. Johnson's interest in literature, Mrs. Mesta's birthday gift to her was a framed photograph of O. Henry with a perfect sentiment for a fifty-year-old woman who does not mind telling her age. Written in the author's own hand was this comforting thought: "The more new wrinkles a woman acquires, the smoother she becomes."

It was one of the nicest parties Lady Bird had ever been to, and protocol went out the window that day. Instead of leaving first, Lady Bird, who was guest of honor, insisted on staying to bid everyone good-bye. Then she presented her gift to Mrs. Mesta. It was a color photograph of herself standing before the mantel at The Elms, Mrs. Mesta's former home. She had written on the picture: "To Perle, from someone who loves living in this house as much as you did."

One Washington "duty" Lady Bird enjoyed so immensely that it could never be called a duty was meeting every Tuesday with the Senate Ladies Red Cross Group to sew or roll bandages for the Bethesda Naval Hospital. It was a January to June pattern for her life during the twelve years her husband was in the Senate, and then, when he became Vice-President, she automatically became President of the Senate Ladies and presided at the weekly sessions. They met at nine o'clock each Tuesday in a large room in the Senate Office Building and exchanged news and views in between stitches, knitting and rolling bandages. Lady Bird was always a "bandage roller" and enjoyed the conversation that went with it, learning what the other Senate wives were doing. She was particularly good about making new people feel at home, and this was one activity at which she was completely relaxed. "It was her quiet time," as one Senate wife described it. Lady Bird says she wishes some historian could have listened in on the conversations because they would have got the inside story of Washington.

In 1957, when the Senate ladies were describing their travels during the Senate recess, Lady Bird told them about her first trip to Paris, in November, 1956. She accompanied her husband, then Democratic leader of the Senate, to a NATO conference composed of parliamentary members of the NATO countries. It was a congenial group that made the trip over in a plane: Senator and Mrs. J. William Fulbright of Arkansas, Senator and Mrs. Thomas Kuchel of California, Senator and Mrs. Carl Curtis of Nebraska, Senator and Mrs. Edmund Thye of Minnesota, Senator Theodore Francis Green of Rhode Island, Representative and Mrs. Homer Thornberry of Texas, and Lyndon and Lady Bird Johnson. In Paris they were joined by Georgia's Senator Richard Russell.

Looking back on the eleven days in France, Lady Bird confesses that "my trip was just for fun only. I did not attend a single session, presuming that I could have, and I brought back no deep and erudite conclusions on the economy, culture and future of France." That was the first and last of her good-time trips with Lyndon, though. She soon discovered that as wife of a dynamic man such as her husband she had a mission to be his "eyes and ears," to learn more about people in every land, about their problems, aims and aspirations, as a means of promoting international friendship, good will and peace. Now that she realizes what that mission is, she fulfills it completely every time.

She looks back on her twenty-four years as a congressional wife with affection and amusement. "I have often thought that congressional wives who drive each year the long stretch between Washington and home—wherever it is—with small children and animals could write a book or movie. *The Perils of Pauline* would be tame in comparison," she said recently.

Indelible in her memory was one particular time she and Lyndon drove those 1,600 miles between Washington and Austin with a cat whose only ambition was to get out, a three-year-old child who was carsick, and a six-year-old who kept asking every mile of the way, "Are we almost in Texas, Mama?"

She remembers also the story of one harassed congressional wife who returned from home to Washington to find a desk piled high with letters to be answered and bills to be paid. She tackled it—and a few days later her kindly but frustrated banker called to say that she had signed all her checks "Love, Mary."

Lady Bird faced her own emergencies too. Before one wartime dinner party she and Lyndon were giving at the time so long ago when butter was rationed, she discovered on short notice that she was out of both butter and ration points with which to buy more. She got on the telephone the afternoon before the dinner and sent an S O S to some guests. It worked. That night when the wife of a Supreme Court justice walked in the door, she held out her right hand to greet her hostess and with her left hand deftly slipped a pound of butter from under her cape to Lady Bird's other hand. Just as deftly, Lady Bird slipped it back to the kitchen, and there was real butter on the plates when the guests sat down to eat. They didn't know how close they came to not having it.

When Lyndon Johnson came to Washington in 1937 as the new congressman from Texas, bringing Lady Bird with him, they settled in an apartment, but in five years they moved ten times. That was just too much for Lady Bird who longed for a home to call her own, so she began to house hunt. She found an attractive white brick two-story house with attic and basement in a neighborhood just a few blocks off fashionable Connecticut Avenue, and after deep deliberations they bought it. This was early in World War II days before real estate prices sky-rocketed in Washington, and they lived there for nearly twenty years, until he became Vice-President.

Having a house in Washington assured some peace of mind to the young congressional wife, but it did not solve the moving problem. Lady Bird spent two weeks out of every year in a frenzy of sorting, packing, shipping and unpacking as she moved the family to Texas each summer, and back again to Washington for the opening of the new session of Congress in the fall or winter. There were innumerable decisions to be made each time: what to lock up and store; what to take to Texas; should the cook go with them or remain in Washington; how would they move Lucy Baines' puppy and, most of all, what to do with the house. "There was only one answer to suit the budget, and that was: it must be rented. Sometimes I think my idea of being rich is not having to rent the house," she once remarked.

When Lady Bird came to Washington in 1937 as a congressional wife, everything was governed by protocol.

Most wives of newly elected officials started out the year buying Carolyn Hagner Shaw's *Green Book*, a social guide to Washington that listed persons prominent socially and in government. Mrs. Shaw told them what they needed to know about the business of making official calls—and it was a business in those early days. A congressional wife called on the wives of the Supreme Court justices on Mondays; on other (mostly senior) congressional wives on Tuesdays; on Cabinet wives on Wednesday, on Senate wives on Thursday; on the Diplomatic Corps on Friday; and at the White House any day. Calls were made between four and six o'clock in the afternoon, and the wife left one of her cards for each of the adult ladies of the household on which she called, left one of her husband's cards for the gentleman of the household, and one of his cards for all the ladies.

Mrs. Shaw explained another bugaboo to new congressional wives, the protocol of seating, which is still quite firmly followed in Washington society, although the order of precedence has changed slightly.

Every official had a rank and his wife carried equal status. It ran something like this: first, of course, was the President; then the Vice-President; the Chief Justice of the Supreme Court; the Speaker of the House (this order of precedence was changed by the late President Kennedy so that the Speaker of the House follows the Vice-President, placing the Chief Justice fourth in line); the Cabinet, starting with the Secretary of State and going down through the most recently created cabinet post; the Associate Justices of the Supreme Court; then the Senate and members of the House of Representatives. In case there are several senators at dinner, the one with the longest period of service ranks highest, and the rest of them according to their seniority in the Senate.

One of the rules in the old days also was that no one should leave the party until the highest-ranking guest had departed. Lady Bird recalls one luncheon where the ranking guest was a brand-new Senate wife. She did not know the rules and stayed and stayed while the rest of the guests fidgeted, thinking about a dentist appointment for a child, or the time they had to pick the children up at school. "We might have been there all afternoon if one of the older ladies had not finally realized the difficulty and whispered in her ear."

Those days, adds Lady Bird, are fortunately past. The war brought too many serious problems for protocol to rule the city, and though it still exists, it is in a modified and more sensible form. Today at a dinner party it is not uncommon for a young congressional wife to walk up to the wife of the Chief Justice and say, "I hope you will excuse us for leaving before you, but the baby-sitter absolutely has to go home in fifteen minutes and we just have time to make it."

President and Mrs. Johnson have through their own gracious consideration of their guests taken a lot of the starch out of entertaining at the White House. At a series of dinners for members of the Senate, the dress was business suit for the men and afternoon dress for the ladies, although it was a seated dinner in the State Dining Room. For state functions the Johnsons have specified black-tie instead of the more formal white-tie dress, realizing that white-tie would be a burden to some of their busy guests.

She belonged to the Congress Club, organized for wives and daughters of members of Congress to give them a social center in Washington. Lady Bird found its Friday afternoon teas an ideal place to take constituents she wanted to give a taste of Washington's social life. It was at the Congress Club, she recalls, that she met her first "real live ambassador," and it was there she studied interior decorating, which became her second-favorite hobby (her first is taking movies). She also belonged to the Texas State Society, and to International Neighbors, a club for wives of members of Congress and diplomats who met regularly to learn better understanding on a person-to-person basis. Also she used to lunch once a month with both the Seventy-fifth Congress Club and the Eighty-first Congress Club, whose members are wives of congressmen elected to the House and Senate in those respective years. She was entitled to membership in both because her husband was elected to the House during the Seventy-fifth Congress, and to the Senate during the Eighty-first Congress.

Over the years, however, Lady Bird grew to love Washington as if it were her real home—not just a part-year residence. The last summer before her husband became the vice-presidential candidate she said, "I adore Washington in the summertime. It changes personality and is so folksy and homey. You can go out to a friend's and eat hamburgers and swim on short notice, or have a dinner at home on the porch for friends from out of town. Just yesterday I enjoyed an informal game of bridge. It has been a long time since I was able to do that."

Occasional outings through the years were Saturday or Sunday drives to Charlottesville, Virginia, to visit Monticello, the home of Thomas Jefferson for whom both her father and her brother were named. Then Lady Bird would take along her two daughters and her niece, Diana MacArthur. They would have lunch or dinner in Warrenton, Virginia, and often stop at antique shops along the way to browse or buy. If she has an opportunity while First Lady, she may include a tour to this historic shrine in the schedule for the wives of some of the state visitors who come to Washington to confer with her husband.

One Christmas not long after he was elected to Congress, her husband gave her a camera and ever since then, movie-making has been her chief hobby. During his unsuccessful campaign for the Senate in 1941 she focused on everything that happened, even turning her camera over to someone else to get movies of his opponent at rallies. She has a complete pictorial record of a luncheon her Congress Club gave for former First Lady Eleanor Roosevelt, but her most cherished film is the pictorial story she has made for her husband's constituents of his achievements down in Texas: flood control, rural electrification and housing.

Another of her hobbies is collecting artifacts, which stems from her history studies at the University of Texas. She has a small bowl made by the Cato Indians who inhabited East Texas from pre-Columbian time until white men settled there in the nineteenth century, and a large, well-preserved Indian pottery bowl, both presented by a Marshall, Texas, plumber who digs artifacts as a hobby and found them near Marshall. She has a vase from Cyprus, given to her by G. L. Clerides, president of the Cyprus House of Representatives, on her visit to Nicosia in 1962. This piece, dating from around 1200 B.C., was unearthed in an ancient tomb near Morphus and is engraved and glazed. Her collection also contains a small vase she got in Italy, and a Roman whale lamp, once used with wick and oil, that came from the archeological museum in Jerusalem.

The most significant indication of the change that has occurred in her life since she became First Lady is in her mail. There is much more of it, and the postmarks are no longer primarily from Texas towns with picturesque-sounding names like Clear Water, Crystal Springs, Sweet Water—names she has always loved because they tell the story of what the early settlers sought and found as they rode across those arid Texas plains.

Now her mail brings letters from around the world: from a Japanese student who wants her to stop the atomic tests; from a church bazaar in Winnepeg asking her to donate one of her hats; and letters from men, women and children all over the United States. A woman in Anniston, Alabama, wrote: "Dear Mrs. Johnson, Heaven bless you for your recipe for corn bread dressing. I saw it in the New Orleans *Picayune* and cut it out to use. I am a Tar Heel and Mama used the same recipe but I didn't get the old cookbooks. I love you and your charming family. Come to Alabama sometime."

A Baltimore minister sent her a poem she inspired him to compose. Titled *Ode to Lady, Lady Bird Johnson*, it began: "Like a pink pearl set in a frame of gold is Lady, Lady Bird Johnson"; a Texan whom Lyndon helped during his first year in Congress wrote: "Dear Claudia," to tell her how proud he is of her husband; a Brooklyn parochial school wrote: "God bless you. Thank you so much for your contribution to our School Music Club's Mardi Gras Festival." A Fayetteville, Tennessee, woman sent her a picture of a filly colt that was named "Lady Bird" for her. Mrs. Johnson replied she was glad to have a real Tennessee walking horse named after her and sent "a few lumps of sugar for your Lady Bird." A woman from Minnesota wrote she was nicknaming her baby daughter "Lady Bird." Mrs. Johnson wrote back that she had had horses and dogs named for her and was pleased to have a little girl named for her at last.

Letters that showed particular appreciation of the job her husband was doing she often kept out and put at his bedside for him to read. She would tell the writer of such a letter that she was doing this because she felt her husband would like to read it. She promised to keep for rereading on special occasions a letter from Mrs. Eugene McCarthy. Abigail McCarthy sent a copy of a speech she had made to a women's group in North Dakota, citing Mrs. Johnson as an example of the women in public life who have grown to accept a new kind of responsibility, and added: "She has done it superbly well."

Mrs. Johnson replied that she was going to keep the letter and speech to reread on those days "when it rains, the plumbing goes out, and Lyndon sends out a hundred constituents unannounced."

Over the years Mrs. Johnson has become a compulsive scrapbook keeper and has twenty-nine gold-tooled leather-bound volumes of family photographs on the bookshelves in the First Family's private sitting room on the second floor of the White House. She wrote her own introduction to the series: "These are scenes from my life, all along the miles and milestones, which Lyndon and I are saving for our children."

Actually the pictures with captions written by Lady Bird tell the story of their life together. The first picture is of Lyndon Johnson as a handsome young man with dark wavy hair in an informal shirt-sleeve pose. He gave the picture to Lady Bird just before they became engaged in 1934. It is followed by the picture of him inscribed: "For Bird, a lovely girl with ideals, principles, intelligence and refinement from her sincere admirer"; a picture of Lyndon and Lady Bird taken on their honeymoon at Lake Xochimilco in Mexico in November, 1934; a picture of Lyndon's first boss, Congressman Richard Kleberg, inscribed: "To my tried and loyal friend with my sincere affection and best wishes from his friend, Richard Kleberg"; and two pictures of the rest of the staff in Congressman Kleberg's office at that time: Gene Latimer and L. E. Jones. It is autographed: "From your boys."

Included also are an autographed picture of Maury Maverick, dated 1935 and inscribed: "To Lyndon Johnson who got me started"; a picture of their "old friend and good wedding arranger," Dan Quill of San Antonio; an autographed picture of Lyndon's boss when he was Texas State Director of NYA, Aubrey Williams; an autographed picture his NYA staff gave him, inscribed: "To our beloved chief, Lyndon Johnson, with highest regards and admiration. NYA boys"; and a picture of Lyndon meeting President Roosevelt in 1937. Two pictures of Lyndon in campaign pose are on facing pages. Under the picture of him standing before a microphone she wrote, "This may influence some voters," and under the opposite picture, of him shaking hands in a hotel lobby, she added, "This surely does; nothing can substitute for the personal touch."

The personal touch is what Lyndon and Lady Bird Johnson have practiced in their many years of political life that led them to the White House.

[V]

Model Mother

Rare is the mother whose children can say they have never seen her angry, but one mother who receives this tribute from her two daughters is Lady Bird Johnson.

"You can't make her mad," declares Lynda Bird, her elder daughter. "She is a lot like Melanie in *Gone With the Wind*, except with more drive. I have never seen her lose her temper. If I get mad at Lucy for taking my hair dryer, or something, Mother says, 'Don't fuss at her, be calm.' "

This is the example Mrs. Lyndon B. Johnson sets for her two daughters—Lynda Bird, who was twenty on March 19 of this year, and Lucy Baines, who is sixteen. And their respect and devotion to their parents, their dignity and behavior as teen-agers, and their consideration and thoughtfulness of others are testimony of the training she has given them.

Although the girls moved into the White House at an impressionable age—an age at which the glamor of the surroundings could easily turn their heads—their mother has no fear it will spoil them. Throughout the years she has taught them not to feel important because of their father's position but to have respect for his job. Her creed for them and for herself has been, "It is the job that is important, not you and I." Sometimes she thinks they may have learned the lesson too well, because once they told her they were "deprivileged" children because their father had too little time for them and they had to live part of each year in Washington when they would rather be in Texas.

"I know there have been a good many times when they wished their father would come home reliably at six o'clock and sit down at the dinner table rather than be gone so much," Mrs. Johnson says. "But now, I really think, they have some sense of the great opportunities and wonderful things that are given to them, as well as some of the difficulties."

Mrs. Johnson says her role is to serve as "balm, sustainer, and sometimes critic for my husband," and also to "help my children look at his job with all the reverence it is due; help them get from it all the knowledge their unique vantage point gives them; and help them retain the light-heartedness to which every teen-ager is entitled."

She will not do this, however, with a set of rules and regulations. She has never disciplined or taught them that way. Instead, she has taken a positive approach, set an example, let them know what is expected, told them she has faith in them and their judgment, and their response has been pleasing.

"My own recipe for raising them is to give them a

considerable sense of independence and to let them know I trust them a lot, but that I am there to see what comes through. It has been very rewarding—so many good things are happening. I'm finding the teens are the most delightful part of our lives together. I don't have a single bad thing to say about the teens which, as I must say, I had feared because of the things I had heard."

Her husband says, "She trusts her children implicitly and they know it. She doesn't nag them, but when they seek her advice, she sounds like a judge weighing all sides, and then she lets them find the answer."

"I know a lot about mothers," he adds. "I thought I had the best one in the world. And I've seen a lot of mothers as a teacher. But I never knew one I thought was more devoted, yet more reserved, than Bird."

Mrs. Johnson never had to resort to spanking to get her children to obey. A look of disapproval from her or their father, or an obvious lack of interest in or enthusiasm for what they were doing brought a quick mending of their ways and an apology from the offender.

The basis for this type of training and discipline is love. One friend observed that the last thing the girls would want is to disappoint their parents or lose their faith and respect. Lynda, deeply serious, expressed it this way: "Mother never tells us to be in from a party or date at a certain time. She just leaves it to our good judgment. How can you break faith with a woman who does that?"

As with so many families who are in politics and public life, Mr. Johnson's responsibilities through the years have taken him and Mrs. Johnson away from home a great deal. On these occasions, the girls were left in the care of Willie Day Taylor, a long-time family friend and a member of Mr. Johnson's staff. She became almost a second mother and the girls affectionately called her "Wil-Day."

Both girls are affectionate and demonstrative, as are their parents, so there is a great deal of actual love shown in the home notwithstanding the guests. Neither Lynda or Lucy is the least bit inhibited about telephoning their parents just to tell them how much they love them.

Likewise, Mrs. Johnson has a habit of ending her telephone calls with such tender remarks as "You are loved" or "I have faith in you," reassuring them they are in their parents' hearts and minds all the time.

"Lucy and I know that whether Mother is with us or not, she is always thinking of us," says Lynda. But on the other hand, the girls do not try to cling to their parents, or keep up with them every minute they are separated. "I don't think you can check up on your parents all the time," Lynda has commented.

Throughout their lives Mrs. Johnson has treated her daughters with adult consideration. She gave each her own bank account and allowance before they entered their teens. She taught them to buy their own clothes within a budget and let them make their own selections within the framework of her guidance. She has taught them public service and responsibility by both example and assignment. As the wife of the Vice-President, she sometimes shared her duties with her daughters. She has let Lucy cut ribbons to open bazaars or flower shows in her place. Last Christmas when she went to the children's wing of D. C. General Hospital to distribute toys the late President and Mrs. Kennedy had bought before his death, she let Lucy take baskets to those in bed too sick to gather in the wards for the presentations made by Mrs. Johnson.

Lynda has traveled abroad with her parents as a teenage good-will ambassador. When her mother visited the Philanthropic Center for Needy Women in Ankara, Turkey, and stopped to take a turn at the knitting machine making gray woolen socks for the Turkish soldiers, Lynda went into the next room and helped sew tiny stitches on a pink-and-white-napkin where workers, of ages ranging from twelve to seventy, were turning out embroidered linens.

Lynda also showed she was a chip off the old block during a motorcade welcoming them to Turkey. As her father stopped the car from time to time along the route, she stepped out and delivered short friendship talks to cheering Turks.

Lynda Bird, who has brown hair, brown eyes and dimples in both cheeks, looks very much like the pictures of her mother when the latter was nineteen, except that Lynda has grown up tall, slim and erect like her father. On the other hand, Lucy is petite, almost fragile-looking, just a fraction shorter than her mother, with light-brown hair, delicate features, blue eyes and an enviable peaches-and-cream complexion. She sometimes wears her hair in a long peekaboo style that not all members of her family and close friends approve, but no one criticizes her. Instead they use the art of praise and persuasion, telling her she has a complexion and profile resembling Princess Grace of Monaco and that she should therefore wear her hair combed back to show off her good features.

Poised as a princess and serious as a statesman, Lynda has had her reigns as royalty. She has been a "Queen" four times, and the last time, when she was Queen of the President's Cup Regatta in Washington, her father made her doubly happy by telling the audience that "she has always been a queen to me." She has also been a Duchess of the Gilmer (Texas) Yam Festival; Queen of the Eighth International Azalea Festival in Norfolk in 1961, and Queen of the Austin Symphony Diamond Ball.

Lynda is more realistic, less of a dreamer than Lucy. Lucy is a much deeper, more thoughtful person than most people think, observing her gay, light-hearted personality. She likes to sew—can whip up a skirt overnight—play the piano, cook and write poetry. She also writes the blessings read at family dinners on such occasions as Christmas, holidays and anniversaries. Her poetry is what one might expect from a much older, more mature person. In contrast to her cheerful personality, her poems have a melancholy note as she writes about "cloudy days" and "deer in the lonely forest." These poems Lucy delights in reading to her friends in somber tones that match the mood of the verse.

Both girls are outgoing, friendly and talkative. Lynda is quick with a quip but never smart-alecky. Lucy lavishes love on pets and people. She has had a series of dogs, ducks, chickens and even white mice. Her pets at the moment are two beagle pups named "Him" and "Her" who are occasionally allowed to frolic in the private family quarters on the second floor of the White House. Lynda's room is decked with stuffed dogs, cats and donkeys. Both girls have a large collection of books and records, but their taste in music varies from year to year so their record collection gets bigger and bigger. Lynda likes bridge (so does her mother and father) and belonged to the bridge club in school.

Lucy has always somewhat resented the fact that she is younger than Lynda, and always wanted the privileges that came to her older sister with each birthday. When Lynda was sixteen, her parents gave her a white convertible. Lucy could hardly wait until she became sixteen so she would get a car of her own—which she did.

Lynda has always taken a maternal attitude toward Lucy but without being bossy. When she was in high school, Lynda set her alarm clock for six-thirty every morning, then spent the next half-hour trying to get Lucy up. Lucy, in turn, who has a talent for hairdressing, often helped her sister with her hair.

Lynda went to charm school to perfect her grace, poise and the art of easy conversation, and Lucy taught herself from what Lynda learned.

Neither Lynda nor Lucy is inclined toward competitive sports as participants, though both love to swim, ride horses and bowl. They learned to water-ski last summer. Both like working with children, and last summer Lucy turned swimming instructor to teach the thirteen-year-old twin sons of the President's long-time assistant, Walter Jenkins, to do all sorts of aquatic tricks in the Johnsons' swimming pool.

Both girls are dignified and mature in thought beyond their years. Both add "sir" or "ma'am" in addressing their elders (Lynda calls her father "sir" more than "Daddy"). They are members of the Episcopal Church in Austin to which their mother belongs. (The President is a member of the Christian Church in Johnson City, Texas, where he joined during a summer revival as a teen-age boy.)

Both girls love clothes and getting dressed up. Lucy leans to feminine things, Lynda prefers classics and tailored dresses, but adores pants and loafers for home wear. Mrs. Johnson says she allows them a great deal of freedom of choice in clothes and other things. She explains, "I want them to have a happy time together, for the years of youth are all too fleeting."

For Lynda and Lucy, life has been divided between two homes bases as long as they can remember: a home in Washington for half the year, and in Texas the other half. When they were in grade school and Congress stayed in session only until July each year, the girls spent half the school year in Austin, where they shared an apartment with Willie Day Taylor. On weekends they joined their parents at the ranch. It was during those years they learned self-reliance and how to get along without leaning on their parents. They studied hard, did their homework without parental help, and made good grades. The other half of the year in their earlier life they went to public school in Washington. Both girls freely admit they would have preferred living in Texas. Of Washington, Lynda has said ruefully, "Life here is geared for congressmen and not their children. The city does not have teen canteens and other places where young people can have fun. It is not a bit like back home in Texas." On another occasion, when someone asked her if she liked her father's ranch in Texas, she replied: "That's like asking whether a cow likes her calf."

Mrs. Johnson feels that living in Washington has its advantages for her children as well as for other congressional children, though they may prefer living in their home state. "Where else could a child grow up hearing in person a State of the Union speech—if she is lucky enough to talk her father out of one of his two prized tickets to the session? Where else is she apt to get served up with dinner the real meat and potatoes of our country—the awareness of what is going on?"

For many years, while they were growing up, both Lynda and Lucy went to Camp Mystic at Hunt, Texas, each summer. "It was almost like belonging to a lodge or sorority," Mrs. Johnson said, "because I have stood in receiving lines all over the country and had mothers tell me their daughters knew my daughters at Camp Mystic."

After grade school, both girls went to a private Episcopal school. Lucy is now a junior at the National Cathedral School in Washington, from which Lynda was graduated in 1962. Lucy wants to go to a college in the Midwest and then be a laboratory technician until she gets married.

Lynda's favorite subject has always been history, which she views through frankly southern eyes. Once, in a high school English composition, she referred to the Civil War as "The War of Northern Aggression." "What do you mean?" demanded her teacher, a Vermonter. "The South fired on Fort Sumter first."

She is a good student who makes better than average

grades. When she enrolled as a freshman at the University of Texas in September of 1962, her ambition was to study history and finally teach it to the fourth and fifth grades until the happy day when she would get married. She found college study a little harder than she had expected. She told her mother, who had graduated from the university twenty-eight years earlier, "You told me if you attended class you made a B, but if you attended class and read the lesson you made an A. It has changed since then. It is much harder than that now." But despite this, Lynda's grades were pleasing—three A's and two B's last year, and she made the honor society.

In her sophomore year, carrying a nineteen-hour class load of English, Latin, history, government, chemistry, and Bible, she continued her good marks. And she was a popular girl on campus. She received invitations from many sororities, but pledged Zeta Tau Alpha at the persuasion of her best friend, who was a Zeta.

The summer between her junior and senior years in high school, Lynda Bird worked as an apprentice at her mother's television station, KTBC, in Austin, learning the ropes from accounting to switchboard operating. She earned a dollar an hour. She opened her own bank account and kept a careful record of every cent she earned and spent. One friend in Austin, noting how hard she worked, asked if she did not miss the social whirl of Washington and perhaps wanted to return to it. "No," she answered brightly. "I want to stay here. Under the new minimum wage law I will make a dollar and fifteen cents an hour after September 1." But in September she had to return to school, so she did not get the increased pay. When her father heard the story he smiled proudly and remarked, "She has a head for business just like her mother."

Lucy says she hates politics but Lynda has always taken an absorbing interest in her father's political career, and when he was in the Senate she frequently telephoned his office to find out how the political battles were going. As a little girl, she used to sit on the knee of the late Speaker Sam Rayburn when he came to the Johnson home to talk politics.

President Johnson has often remarked that "I will never have to worry about either girl. Lynda Bird is so smart she will always be able to make a living for herself. And Lucy Baines is so appealing and feminine there will always be some man around wanting to make a living for her." However, Lynda was the first to become engaged to be married and there was speculation there would be a White House wedding this year. But the engagement was broken by mutual consent last April. Her fiancé was Lieutenant (j.g.) Bernard Rosenbach, whom she met on a blind date in Texas the summer before she was a senior in high school. Bernie, a tall fair-haired youth from Comfort, Texas, which is fifty miles from the LBJ Ranch, was appointed to the Naval Academy by the Secretary of the Navy. They had a good time on that first date, then he invited her to a dance at the Naval Academy and many more followed. Because Bernie could not get away from the Academy as much as he wanted to, Lynda would drive down to Annapolis from Washington to see him. By the time she had graduated in June, 1962, she was wearing the young midshipman's pin. She was there when he graduated from the Naval Academy and was as proud as any girl in Annapolis that day of the new young officer.

That summer Bernie, wearing his new ensign bars, was sent to sea and Lynda went with her parents when they were sent by President Kennedy on a mission to the Middle East. But while the Vice-President and Mrs. Johnson went to Cyprus, Lynda Bird, accompanied by Bess Abell, went to Naples to see her boy friend, whose ship was there.

She joined her parents in Rome and with them had an

audience with Pope John XXIII. When Lynda told him she was pinned to "a Catholic boy," the Pope exclaimed, "Oh, how wonderful!" The Vice-President added, "She'll probably marry him," and His Holiness pronounced his blessings on the proposed union, gave Lynda two matching rosaries—one for her and one for Bernie.

In April of 1963, Bernie wrote a letter to the Vice-President asking for his daughter's hand in marriage.

Secretly he was pleased that the young man of her choice had the old-fashioned courtesy to ask her father's permission for them to become engaged. But he teasingly told Lynda that he was going to tell Bernie that he had to wait until she finished college, got her master's degree and then her doctor's degree before she could marry. Mrs. Johnson tried to ease her daughter's obvious anxiety by citing instances to both her and her father of successful marriages where the girl had finished college after she was married. But he did not relent in his teasing.

The Vice-President gave his reply to the young naval officer, and Lynda's engagement was revealed two months later, in June, at The Elms in Washington. The party was a substitute for the debut Lynda chose not to make, and she had a big hand in planning it, assisted by her mother and the latter's secretary, the capable Bess Abell. They did not know until the last minute, however, whether the Vice-President would reveal his daughter's engagement or not. But they chose a "daisies don't tell" theme that would be appropriate whether he did or not. There were baskets of daisies on all the tables covered with yellow cloths. Daisies trailed from Japanese lanterns hanging in the trees, and a big basket of daisies floated on the swimming pool. Lynda's roommate at the university, Warrie Lynn Smith, came up for the occasion and helped with the planning. Lynda made up the guest list, including, in addition to friends her own age, her pediatrician, some of her teachers and her favorite senators.

Actually it was two parties—an early reception for some hundred and fifty adult friends, and a late supper and dance for fifty of her own age. There was an early buffet for the older crowd, and a spaghetti supper for the younger set. For both there were barbecued spareribs. Lynda had asked Walter Jetton, the Texas barbecue king, to bring his chuck wagon up from Fort Worth to serve his delicious hickory-smoked ribs. A portable dance floor—linoleum sprinkled with cornstarch to give it a dancing polish—was set up on the lawn beside the flagstone patio. Devron's orchestra provided the music for dancing under the stars on this June night, and Lynda had her first dance with her tall, handsome father. Soon he was tapped on the shoulder by equally tall, handsome Ensign Rosenbach who had earlier slipped a diamond ring on her finger. Later that evening the Vice-President stepped to the microphone and in a voice filled with emotion said, "Friends, as the father of daughters, you learn there are many important milestones—the day she was born, the first day she goes to school, and the day she arrives back from college with a young man in hand. I'd like to ask you to join me in toasting Lynda who has been the light of my life for nineteen years and to Bernie whom we have come to know, to admire and to love . . ." The secret was out. Now the daisies could tell and she could wear her diamond ring back to school in September.

President Kennedy's tragic death was a deep personal loss to both the Johnson daughters because he was a special favorite of theirs. He particularly liked to tease Lynda about her boy friends, and after her engagement he threatened several times to ship Ensign Rosenbach to some far-off post with the Navy. Each time it was to some post more remote and distant than the last. But she took it with the smiles and good nature in which it was said.

The girls also adored Mrs. Kennedy, who had invited

them to the White House on various occasions. When she sent them an invitation to a state dinner for the President of Sudan, they thought it was a mistake. Both Vice-President and Mrs. Johnson were out of town, so Lucy penned a note to Mrs. Kennedy saying: "We are very excited to have received the invitations, but we are curious to find out if you know our ages." Back came a reassuring letter from Mrs. Kennedy: "I am very well aware of your ages, but I want you to come anyway." Thrilled at the prospect of being guests at a glamorous state dinner, the two teen-age girls telephoned their mother in Austin and discussed White House deportment. She capsuled her advice in one sentence: "Read all you can find in the encyclopedia about the Sudan, and don't drink any of the wine at dinner."

For the first few days after her father had become President, Lucy had difficulty getting to school on time. When she arrived in her white Convair convertible, a Secret Service agent seated beside her, she was greeted each morning by a flock of photographers who trailed her to the classroom door, begging her to stop or turn around for just one more picture.

"They make me late for class," she complained, then solved the problem herself by getting up fifteen minutes earlier every morning and starting out for school to allow time for the photographers. Then another problem arose. "I wonder how much longer the photographers will be going to school with me? I'm running out of clothes," she confided. She had been wearing a different outfit every day so that the pictures would always be a little different.

Lynda, who had missed one of the most important moments in her father's life—seeing him nominated for the Vice-Presidency—also missed the family's first days in the White House, but this was because she was at college and not by accident.

She was at Disneyland with her best boy friend from

Texas when her father was nominated for the Vice-Presidency at the 1960 Democratic National Convention in Los Angeles. Mrs. Johnson blamed herself, though, for letting Lynda go. After her husband had lost the presidential nomination to John F. Kennedy, it seemed to Mrs. Johnson that the convention held no more promise for Texans, so she decided that Thursday afternoon would be a quiet time for Lynda to go to Disneyland. "That shows what a poor prophet I am," she confessed. Lynda remembers the day vividly. She set off for Disneyland about two in the afternoon. When she arrived, she checked in at the security gate just in case there might be a message for her to return. But there was nothing for her. However, an hour later Senator Kennedy announced he wanted Johnson as his running mate and a frantic search for Lynda began. By that time she was lost among the thousands plunging down the Matterhorn on a bobsled, diving in the submarine, and soaring to Never-Never Land with Peter Pan. And about the time her parents were leaving for the Sports Arena, Lynda was laughing at a vaudeville cancan show at the Golden Horseshoe. Sometime after nine o'clock a waitress at a snack bar told her that Johnson had been nominated for Vice-President. Lynda called the headquarters, and blanched when she found it was true and that there had been broadcasts over the three national networks for her. Fearful but happy she joined her family after the wild ovation for her father in the Sports Arena had died down. She encountered a frowning father who asked sternly: "What did you think we came here for—Disneyland?" The next day Lynda confessed: "I was always Daddy's darling daughter. But I was not Daddy's darling daughter last night."

The following night, however, she was there for the excitement in the Los Angeles Coliseum when both her father and Senator Kennedy made their acceptance speeches. She and Lucy stood by to be introduced, had smiles and waves for the enormous crowds. Months later, she confessed that the boy friend she was with at Disneyland "didn't like all the publicity and I don't see him much now."

The two girls had hoped they would be permitted to campaign for their father, but there was school to return to after summer. So with one or two exceptions, when they went out, they remained at home in Washington with Willie Day Taylor while their mother and father traveled, from sea to shining sea. In Washington they kept up with the campaign and how things were going by watching television and through letters and phone calls from their parents. They were full of suggestions of how to improve their parents' techniques. "Lucy often told me my voice was too loud and shrill when I spoke and that I should keep it soft. And she was right. When I'm under strain I tend to talk loud," Mrs. Johnson said. But in the face of Lucy's criticism, Lynda Bird always defended her mother—said she was doing a good job.

From the letters the girls sent their mother, Mrs. Johnson knew she was needed back in Washington and had a job there to do as soon as the campaign was over. "I've got to do something about their spelling," she said. "One has only to read their letters to know they need remedial spelling."

On election night the girls stayed up until four-thirty in the morning listening to the returns, rooting for their father and Senator Kennedy. But they were up again at six-thirty, getting ready for school, and went to class as usual although their minds were on the election and the winners.

After her father became President, Lynda Bird, a typical American coed, took the presence of a Secret Service man at her side on campus in stride. He caused quite a stir among other girls on the campus, though, who smiled, waved and tried to talk to him at every opportunity. Lynda said, "He sits in class and seems very interested. He's learning things too."

Then Lynda learned that the agents watching her in Texas had homes in Washington and thus had to be separated from their families while protecting her. She quietly began making plans to transfer to a college in the Washington area so she could be at home with her family, and the Secret Service agents could be with theirs. Her thoughtfulness of others pleased her parents very much, and also the fact that they would have her with them at the White House during the final months before her marriage. When she enrolled at George Washington University she brought a Texas friend with her. Warrie Lyn Smith, her roommate at the University of Texas, was invited to come and live at the White House and go to George Washington University also. Thus, Lynda would have a friend and classmate with her.

When the First Family took up official residence in the White House on December 7, Lucy arrived driving her white convertible with her two beagle puppies sired by "Little Beagle," the family's long-time pet famous for getting lost in Washington, and who died last year at the ripe old age of twelve. Mrs. Johnson arrived in a chauffeur-driven limousine carrying a color photograph of the late Sam Rayburn which was hung in the family sitting room. Lynda missed this home-coming because she was at the University of Texas, but her mother conferred with her by long-distance telephone each night to learn how she wanted her room at the Executive Mansion.

She wanted to keep the fruitwood furniture from her bedroom at The Elms and all her cherished possessions: her doll collection, her bookcases of history and biography, her record player and collection of records, her television set and her collection of college banners. Her bedroom was the one formerly occupied by Caroline Kennedy, and she decided to have the walls painted a warm yellow.

Her doll collection, some of them a hundred years old, is her most cherished possession next to the gold cross she wears on a chain around her neck. Both the dolls and the cross were gifts from her father's mother, who died in 1958. Lynda was very close to her grandmother and visited her every summer. She and Lucy called her "Maw-Day," a name they gave her before they could pronounce "grandmother."

Lucy's room at the White House is the one formerly occupied by John F. Kennedy, Jr., but now it is as feminine-looking as she is. It is filled with her own French-type, off-white furniture with a four-poster bed that has a white eyelet-trimmed canopy matching the white coverlet. "Lucy is a blue-and-white, lace-and-ruffles little girl," her mother says.

The White House has much to offer as a place for teen-agers to entertain. It has a theater on the ground floor, where Lynda and Lucy may give theater parties and let their guests see the newest films or old favorites. There is also an indoor swimming pool for year-round swimming, if they can be assured their water-loving father will not want to bring one of his callers in for a dip in the pool at the same time they are giving a swimming party.

After Caroline Kennedy's kindergarten moved out of the third-floor oval room at the White House, Mrs. Johnson decided it should become a recreation room for Lynda and Lucy and their friends. "After all, you can't have a date in the Blue Room," she remarked. The vinyl tile floor was ideal for dancing, and there was a television set, hi-fi, record player and refrigerator. She arranged some comfortable sofas to give it a cozy atmosphere in which the girls and their guests could enjoy themselves. It was in this room that President Truman gave breakfast parties when he was in the White House, and President and Mrs. Eisenhower held card parties there.

Extra guests at their parties now, at home and away,

may well be Secret Service agents keeping a protective eye on the President's daughters. Lucy learned early that dating as the President's daughter is never a private twosome. On her second Sunday in the White House, a young midshipman from the Naval Academy took her to a Washington restaurant for dinner. But they could not go in like an ordinary couple. First, two Secret Service agents had to inspect the restaurant. After they gave their okay, one remained behind in the car while the other followed Lucy and her date inside. As they dined he sipped coffee at a nearby table, out of earshot but close enough to watch them.

"It doesn't exactly breed romance, you know," Lynda has quipped of the chaperons. She recalls one occasion during the inauguration when Lucy's boy friend was trying to give her his senior ring and had a very awkward time of it with the Secret Service watching her every second.

Secret Service protection will cost Lucy Baines some earned money too. Before she moved into the White House she supplemented her five-dollar-a-week allowance by addressing envelopes, baby-sitting for friends, and selling the brownies she bakes so expertly, to friends. Now she has a valid argument for a bigger allowance: she can't very well keep on baby-sitting with a Secret Service agent tagging along to watch her.

Although each girl has an income of several hundred dollars a month from investments their parents have made for them, the money is not theirs to spend, and they must get along on a weekly allowance. When they were in grade school, they got fifty cents a week each. Out of this, Lynda, who is thrifty like her mother, could save money. Lucy sometimes splurged the whole amount the first day, but as their allowance increased with their age, Lucy learned economy. Now if she wants more money, she works for it, and spends it wisely.

The first evening Lynda returned home her parents were giving an informal dinner for members of the Senate and their wives, and she very gracefully walked into the State Dining Room, kissed her father warmly and took a seat behind him and Mrs. Gale McGee on his left. They chatted happily a few minutes. Then she moved her chair next to her mother, who was seated between Senator McGee and Senator Thomas Dodd.

It was the natural sort of thing she would have done had her parents been entertaining guests at the LBJ Ranch or in their previous homes in Washington.

[VI]

A Brain for Business

Petite, feminine Lady Bird Johnson does not look like a big business executive who parlayed a modest inheritance into a multimillion dollar enterprise in the highly competitive broadcasting industry, but she is and she did. She is not only one of the most astute businesswomen in the United States; she is the first millionaire First Lady who earned her fortune herself. She did it by hard work, shrewd investing and sheer luck.

This is a facet of Lady Bird's life that rarely comes into public focus though, because she does not talk much about her business accomplishments. Lady Bird did much of the work in her Washington home with periodic flying trips to Texas to assess and tackle operational problems, or to preside over meetings of the staff or board of the LBJ

Company, owner of radio and television stations, of which she was chairman.

Until her husband went to war in 1941, and she ran his congressional office for eight months, Lady Bird was not sure she could make a living for herself if it became necessary. She had ambitions and dreams but little self-confidence. But in meeting the everyday challenges and problems of a congressman as she did, she acquired an assurance and experience that gave her an appetite for more challenges. Thus, when he returned from the war in August, 1942, she was reluctant to go back to her former role of just being a congressional wife, and they had no children then to demand her time. She began to wish for something challenging she could do. Also, she wanted a business of their own that might one day be a cushion in case her husband decided to step out of politics. She wanted to buy a newspaper and had even picked the one she wanted in Texas, but it cost too much for her. Then she heard about a small radio station in Austin with dual ownership that was to be sold, and she looked into its potentials. About that time, too, she received a portion of her mother's estate which her father had been holding for her. There was a decision to be made on what to do with that money.

In all she got about $67,000, but at that particular time she got $21,000. With that $21,000 and a $10,000 loan from the bank, she negotiated for the purchase of KTBC, the small debt-ridden radio station in Austin, Texas, which was losing nearly $2,000 a month. It was several months later—February, 1943, to be exact—that the Federal Communications Commission granted approval of the sale, and Lady Bird was in business. She went to Austin to take over her new property—and she stayed on the job full-time until August.

There was much for her to learn. Problems cropped up almost hourly, demanding immediate action. And the desperate effort to stem the tide of losses went on day after day. One of the first things she did was to get soap and a bucket of water and get to work cleaning up the place. She then got down to business, searching through all the ledgers, contracts and operational reports to find the answers to why the station was losing money and how to stop it. These were not entirely strange documents to her. She was slightly familiar with profit-and-loss statements and contractural procedures. From the time she was twelve years old her mother's bachelor brother, Claude Patillo, for whom she was named, had been sending her books on property management, bookkeeping and business methods to prepare her for the day when she would inherit the wealth he had acquired in Alabama and which he planned to bequeath to his namesake. She read all the books he sent. He also cherished a hope that she might one day go to the Harvard School of Business and become a successful businesswoman. She didn't go to Harvard, but she lived up to his expectations as a businesswoman although he didn't live to see her accomplishments, for he died in 1941.

In Austin, Lady Bird worked long hours to learn about the operation of the radio station which at the time she bought it had no network affiliation, no night time and only nine employees. She first tackled the so-called "bad debts" and right there found a clue to some problems. She came across one for the Kellogg Cereal Company. "That can't be," she thought. "Kellogg is too big to have a bad debt." She asked the manager for the contract. It called for five spots a week, but the station had run six and sent an invoice for six. Kellogg paid for five. "That's not their mistake; we'll have to scratch that one off the books," she said. She went through the entire list of debtors and ascertained what was valid and what was inaccurate. She got the books straightened out. Then she turned her attention to the employees, evaluated each for his contribution to the business and ability to do his job. She decided she needed a new manager and got one. She stayed on just the same, working night and day for five months until finally, in August, the station showed a profit of $18. From that time on the profit chart showed an upward trend.

In the meantime, Lyndon Johnson had stayed on his job in Washington, busily backing wartime legislation requested by President Roosevelt. Regardless of how hard he worked he missed Lady Bird. He wanted her there to hear his problems and share with him his hard-won triumphs, but most of all he just wanted her near him.

They had brief reunions when she returned to Washington or he went to Austin to see her. Other times they bridged the miles with letters and telephone calls that seemed all too brief, infrequent and inadequate. In Lady Bird's scrapbook today is one particularly plaintive letter he wrote to her on May 7, 1943, underscoring how much he needed and missed her. He wrote:

> Dearest Lady Bird,
>
> I'm writing a letter to Mother for Mother's Day and I wish you would be a good girl and go down and buy her a suitable present. You know what she would like a lot better than I, so just use your own judgment.
>
> If you don't start writing me more often I am going to have you drafted into the WAACs. Then you'll *have* to write your next of kin at least twice a month.
>
> Had dinner with Bill Douglas last night and he was his usual entertaining self. He wished that you could have been there, but not half as much as
>
> Your Congressman
> Lyndon B. Johnson

When Lady Bird returned to Washington in August she was jubilant over her success in putting the station in the black even if by such a small margin as $18. This was cause enough for celebration. But there was even better news.

She learned she was going to have a baby—their first child. The following March 19 Lynda Bird was born, the baby they had wanted for such a long time. Her cup of happiness was runing over, and her hands were really full. But she learned to manage her time as efficiently as she managed her money. One long-time friend said, "The reason she can do as much as she does is because she plans her time so well. I know of no one who plans the utilization of their time as efficiently and intelligently." She kept up with duties as a congressional wife, still taking constituents on sightseeing tours of Washington, took care of her little girl, and kept watch over the flourishing business in Austin. By 1945 the assets of the station for which she had paid $30,000 were listed at $78,001.

Luck played a heavy hand in Lady Bird's favor when the Federal Communications Commission allotted TV channels to Austin. The LBJ Company applied for and received Channel 7. The FCC gave Austin one very-high-frequency channel and two ultra-high-frequency channels. In those days it was impossible to know whether the future of television lay in UHF or VHF stations. The only other Austin applicant asked for a UHF station. Just on a guess, Lady Bird requested the VHF. And she guessed right, because television sets were made to receive only VHF stations and people did not buy converters to tune in the UHF channels.

With both a television station and a radio outlet in bustling Austin, profits for the LBJ Company soared. There was more money to invest and the corporation began to buy into radio and television stations in other towns. At the time she became First Lady and placed her broadcasting properties in a trusteeship until her husband was out of federal office, the LBJ Company owned

29.05 per cent of KWTX-AM-TV in Waco, Texas, and this station's holdings included 50 per cent in a satellite TV station in Bryan, Texas, and 75 per cent of KXII-TV in Ardmore, Oklahoma. Two years earlier, the LBJ Company had sold a radio and television station in Weslaco, Texas, for $1.4 million.

And at the time she placed her properties in trusteeship to allay any suggestions of conflict of interest, the total worth of Lady Bird's broadcasting holdings was variously estimated as high as $5 million. She held 53 per cent of the stock in the LBJ Company and Lynda Bird, then nineteen, and Lucy Baines, sixteen, owned slightly more than 30 per cent, their interest also in a trusteeship.

Every Saturday morning for years before she moved into the White House, a large manila envelope would arrive at the Johnson home in Washington addressed to Lady Bird. It contained a complete account of the week's activities of the Austin radio and television stations, the only ones in which she had a personal hand in the management. Then for the next few hours after its arrival, she stepped out of her role as Washington wife and became a Texas business executive taking the financial pulse of her corporation.

Each salesman for the stations made a report to her, listing every call he had made during the week, the pitch he gave the merchant and the response he got. There was also a daily account showing the amount of money received for the time sold each day of the week. This she compared with the same period of the preceding month and the previous year. "It gives you a graph of how you are doing," Mrs. Johnson explained recently. "But it makes no sense until you look on the other side of the sheet and see whether your expenses are rising or not. That margin to the business person is the real gauge to how well you are doing."

From these reports she could also tell how things were going in the entire business community in Austin—whether the merchants were feeling sanguine or not.

Under her guidance over the past twenty years the business has grown from 9 to 104 employees; from no network to a CBS affiliation and some hours with NBC and ABC; from 250 to 5,000 watts of power; and from a poor news service to what Mrs. Johnson calls " a sizable staff of topnotch people." This success, she modestly contends, is not due to any extraordinary qualities as a businesswoman or a broadcaster on her part but rather to good judgment.

"If you are able to use good judgment, that is half the battle," she says. "Then you must have good people around you and you must keep them. We are fortunate in that respect. Our employees have been with us for years. We have a retirement and insurance program and also a profit-sharing plan."

One of the first people she hired after taking over the station, Paul Bolton, is still with her. He is now news director. In 1946, she picked as her general manager Jesse C. Kellam, former deputy state superintendent of public instruction, who took leave from that job to work with Lyndon Johnson when he was Texas State Administrator for the National Youth Administration. Kellam, who succeeded Johnson as NYA Administrator, is now president as well as general manager of the LBJ stations.

No detail of the stations' operation was too small for Mrs. Johnson's attention. And as new employees were added, she tried to get to know each one personally and evaluate the potential contribution they might make to the business. When anyone did a good job—even if no more than writing a particularly illuminating report—she was quick to praise. She was always thinking of little extras to make life easier, more enjoyable for her staff. She allowed them to spend free weekends and vacations at one of the Johnson ranch houses in the Texas hill country south of Austin. If she happened to be at the LBJ Ranch at the time, she would drop in to see them and bring them little gifts. She took an interest in the personal lives of her employees; when someone had a new baby she sent a check in the baby's name to start a bank account for the new arrival. Because many of her executives were pilots, she had the company buy three airplanes for them to use in flying to New York, Washington, Atlanta or Dallas in search of business. Today, the fleet has been reduced to a single twin-engine, nine-passenger Beechcraft Queen-Aire which Mrs. Johnson bought recently, trading in the three other planes and paying a $90,000 tab.

She boasts that one of her best salesmen is a woman. But Lady Bird is not a feminist in the strictest sense of the word. She says, "The great effort of women is not, I believe, to invade a man's world or to create a woman's world but to be a full operating partner in a warm compassionate world."

Her business associates see as one important clue to her success the fact that she "makes people want to do their best and she inspires them toward this end." She is quick to make a decision. She has limitless patience to hear the pros and cons of each question; then when she has the full facts she reaches her decision promptly because she has weighed each fact as it was presented.

If she is asked to make a decision between bigger profits for the company or giving the listeners what they want, she will rule in favor of the listeners. She did just that recently when station officials were debating whether to give the final news broadcast of the evening at ten or eleven o'clock. Scheduling it at eleven would have given an extra hour of prime time, of vast commercial value. But she found her listeners preferred the news an hour earlier. That is what she ordered.

She has said she believes that radio and television stations have a public service status "and no operation can be truly profitable or successful unless the operator keeps that in mind."

Although she has always had the final decision on programming and policy making, in recent years she has taken an increasing interest in her stations' programs and boasts of their abundance of news and weather reports. "Weather news in Texas is our staff of life because of our agriculture," she says. "Besides that our TV station carries seventeen out of the twenty most popular programs on the CBS network, not necessarily because they appeal to our more sophisticated viewers, but because we want to give them what they want to see."

She is a firm believer in keeping it a "local-station operation" because "we believe we can stimulate more people into realistic, constructive thought about their area problems and the future." This philosophy was behind two special program series of which she is especially proud. One was called *Insight* and the other *Project Seven.* One of these programs presented Dr. Edward Teller, originator of the hydrogen bomb, in an interview with qualified local people to explain the advances in nuclear development and use. Another explained the vital importance of the SAC bases, the necessity for constant training flights with the admittedly disturbing noise as the planes break the sound barrier, and why it is imperative to keep this up.

One of the most successful programs on *Insight*, she said recently, was the appearance of four criminals from the Texas penitentiary whose crimes ranged from theft to murder. They told their life stories on camera and what caused them to engage in crime. They were questioned by a panel of teen-agers. It brought tremendous listener response and praise from the community, and Texas prison authorities asked for prints to show before various groups.

Even if a solution to a local problem isn't proposed, Mrs. Johnson is especially desirous that a program nudge local leaders and citizens in the community to take action toward finding an answer. One program of this type was titled *Why the Young Man Left Town.* "I know people think about Texas as a place of widespread prosperity, but we have towns that offer no future for young people and off they go to California," she explains.

She keeps her ear tuned to community reaction to programs, and her managers meet at regular intervals with an advisory board, made up of representatives from such groups as P. T. A., the Ministerial Alliance and the University of Texas. "We are interested in their views, and though we don't always follow their advice, we listen to what they say," she says. She orders frequent listener surveys to see if her station is giving Austin what it wants on radio and television.

In 1959 Lady Bird decided it was time for her Austin broadcasting business to move into a home of its own. Since 1943 the business had been operating in rented, inadequate quarters, and as a result of the growth the desks were almost piled on top of one another. During the last four months of 1959 and the first four months of 1960, she flew to Texas frequently to supervise the construction of the modern eight-floor building that would have an apartment for her to occupy when in Austin. At other times it would be available for visiting clients. Interior decorating is one of Lady Bird's main hobbies and she looked forward to planning the décor for the apartment and the building. But in the summer of 1960 those dreams were shattered when her husband was chosen the vice-presidential nominee. Instead of decorating the interior of her new building first-hand, she toured the country decorating political platforms to win votes for the Democratic ticket. Every time she passed through Austin she slipped away to the new building to see how her ideas were taking shape under the guidance of someone else.

Somehow in her busy campaign travels she found time to select every piece of furniture that went into the $800,000 building. She planned the décor of the fifth-floor apartment that has a color scheme of blue, green and beige. The rugs are beige, the walls blue-green, and on one wall is a mural of an island that reminds her, she says, "of the faraway places and strange-sounding names I may never get to see in person." The furniture in the apartment is modified modern, a contrast to the early-American style at the LBJ Ranch and the traditional décor at their home in Washington.

Not being there to attend to the last details of the building, she felt, was like "having your daughter get married and not be there to help select the wedding dress."

Though Lady Bird is modest about her achievements as a businesswoman, her husband often boasts that "Bird is the brains and money of this family." She accepts this jocular assertion with a smile and a pat on her husband's head to show where she thinks the brains are. But her talents as a businesswoman are recognized beyond her own family circle. For her achievement and leadership in broadcasting Lady Bird has won two outstanding honors in recent years. She won a gold-framed salute from Theta Sigma Phi, honorary sorority for women in journalism, for her own "professional endeavors in radio and journalism and for inspiring increased respect for women's capabilities both in this country and abroad." The American Women in Radio and Television awarded her a citation in 1963 "in appreciation of her contribution to the broadcasting industry as a distinguished executive mindful of her responsibilities to her community and to her stations," and made her honorary chairman of Project One of the Educational Foundation of AWRT.

In accepting this award from the AWRT, Lady Bird called on the women in radio and television and all their male colleagues to use the facilities at their command to help others around the world: to bring to the underdeveloped parts of the world the cumulative knowledge in science, agriculture, medicine, as well as cultural forms; to use this country's knowledge in child care so that infant mortality around the world will be reduced; to share with Asia and Africa our knowledge of how to grow more corn and wheat so that the bread baskets of the world will be full and there will be no empty stomachs; to take our TV medical heroes and use them as a conduit for bringing to others the knowledge that will help to eliminate tuberculosis, typhoid fever, and other diseases.

"It is through sharing the benefits of our way of life that our way of life will survive," she said.

Mrs. Johnson's business interests have extended beyond the bounds of broadcasting. She also owns rental property in Austin, which was purchased before she acquired the radio station, and 3,800 acres of land in Autauga and Chilton counties in Alabama which she inherited from her mother's family. The wealth Lady Bird Johnson has acquired provided a new way of life for her family long before they moved into the White House. It was, of course, not necessary to practice the frugality that marked the early years of her marriage, when she did her own cooking and housekeeping. But frugality is a habit now, and even as the wife of the President she rides air-shuttle service from Washington to New York rather than going first class, just as she used to buy balcony seats instead of orchestra at the theater to save money, and one Christmas she asked her husband for a tool kit so that she could make small repairs around the house.

"Lyndon wants me to handle everything I am capable of handling," she says. "He is a little incensed if I want help on trivial things. I feel sometimes he thinks I am more capable than I am—which in a way makes me grow to be a little more capable." She paid all the household bills, kept tax records and signed checks for the radio-TV stations too before the business was placed in trusteeship. Much of the work she did at her desk at home, but it was not uncommon to see her in Washington going to the beauty shop or the dentist's office carrying a large colorful Mexican straw bag filled with books to read in spare moments, business reports to digest and checks to sign.

Now, as chatelaine of the 132-room White House where operating costs come to some $680,000 a year, she practices the same thrift and budgetary rules that have marked her business endeavors with success. Running the presidential mansion is no part-time job. The regular domestic and maintenance staff numbers about seventy-five and Mrs. Johnson likes to take a personal interest in each employee. She maintains that this gives each a sense of pride in his or her work.

In addition to three domestic staff members she brought with her from The Elms—Mrs. Zephyr Wright, the family cook; Mrs. Helen Williams; and Mrs. Lee Gregg—the regular domestic force at the White House consists of a maître d'hôtel, two housekeepers, four butlers, six cooks, a valet, five doormen, five housemen, a head laundress—who sends the linens out to a commercial cleaner—a pantry woman and eight maids.

To keep the mansion in good shape, there is a maintenance crew of eight engineers, four carpenters, four electricians, three plumbers, two storekeepers, a painter and about ten helpers and handy men. Eleven gardeners maintain the eighteen acres of ground in an operation that comes under the United States Park Service.

[VII]

Political Campaigner

President Johnson calls her his "Madison Avenue"; Adlai Stevenson describes her as both "beguiling and efficient"; and Democratic professionals term her the Party's "Secret Weapon." They all mean the same thing: Lady Bird Johnson is an effective campaigner with a deft touch that wins votes. She is undoubtedly the best feminine speaker the Party has.

She is credited with swinging the Texas vote to the Kennedy-Johnson ticket in the 1960 presidential election and with saving some other Southern states for the Democrats. She helped swell the Democratic vote in many traditionally G. O. P. territories of the North, and spread Southern charm in silk-stocking Republican districts in New York City.

Lady Bird set a new record for feminine campaigning in the 1960 election. She traveled 35,000 miles in 71 days on behalf of the Kennedy-Johnson ticket. She said a few well-chosen words—she refused to call them speeches—before 200 gatherings in those 71 days; she made 16 campaign appearances in 11 states on her own; attended 16 joint campaign receptions with the sisters of the presidential candidate, John F. Kennedy; made some 150 appearances with her husband; and gave 65 "greeting" talks from the back platform of a campaign train that chugged its way through Dixie.

She also held more press conferences in two months than most Presidents hold in a year, and two of her conferences were held in governors' offices—something new for a candidate's wife.

Once so shy that she prayed she would not have to make the valedictory address, Lady Bird felt this timidity disappear on the campaign trail. "The way you overcome shyness," she explains, "is to become so wrapped up in something that you forget to be afraid. Lyndon expects a lot of me, so I have learned not to be afraid any more."

The kick-off of her role in the campaign was at a press conference—her first—on August 23, 1960, in familiar surroundings, the Woman's National Democratic Club in Washington, and with flying colors she sailed through the questions of a couple of dozen women reporters. She had not planned to go into campaign issues, but the questions came up and she did not duck them. She had learned her lesson, though, and the answers she gave, seemingly on the spur of the moment, had the ring of a true politician's. One of the first questions was about the religion of the presidential candidate.

"Sadly, there is such a thing as a religious issue," Lady Bird answered in a soft, almost hurt voice. "But the more deeply one reads the Bible and the more one thinks about it, the fairer one will be. I hope in the final analysis, after thinking things over and thinking real hard, voters will size the candidate up on the basis of how devoted a leader he is."

However, she added with a tone of fight in her voice, if the Democratic ticket "runs into real trouble" on the issue of religion in Texas, "Lyndon has plenty of blood-kin Baptists" to call on for help. His great-grandfather was president of Baylor University and there were several Baptist ministers among his ancestors, one of them George Washington Baines, who "converted Sam Houston to the Church."

Mrs. Johnson announced her first campaign trip: to Texas, where a series of coffee and tea parties and receptions would be held, at which she would introduce Mrs. Sargent Shriver, sister of Mr. Kennedy, and Mrs. Robert F. Kennedy, whose husband was campaign manager for the presidential candidate. "I'm going to be very proud to show Texas off to these two very attractive members of Senator Kennedy's family and very proud to introduce them to Texas," Lady Bird added.

When she arrived in Texas with Mrs. Shriver and Mrs. Robert Kennedy for their flying tea party across the state, Lady Bird's little entourage was met by about fifty citizens—mostly women—and it was apparent that it would be a difficult mission to capture women's votes for the Democratic ticket. But the "Kennedy women," as Lady Bird referred to them, turned on their charm and made newspaper headlines with their answers to questions about the presidential candidate, and as word got out that Lady Bird was there, the crowds began to swell. They were joined later by another Kennedy sister, Pat Lawford, wife of movie star Peter Lawford, and by the vice-presidential candidate himself, Lyndon Johnson. The crowds turned almost into mobs. Often Lyndon would order a man with muscles to run interference through the crushing crowds while he followed behind Lady Bird, his arms protectively encircling her from behind.

There were other trips across Texas for Lady Bird, both

with Lyndon and without him. In all, she stumped across the state four times in that campaign and proved to be a popular campaigner with the men as well as with the women. She was the brighest spot in the campaign. She breezed across Texas like a prairie fire—a petite, vibrant figure always dressed in red. She stood on tiptoe to reach the microphones, set up on hurridly erected platforms in parking lots at shopping centers, to beg Texas voters to support a native son—her husband—for Vice-President.

One morning in a Fort Worth hotel she balanced a plate of cold pancakes on her knee as she telephoned a speech to be taped and played back at a Democratic women's luncheon in Brown, Texas. That was part of her schedule in the campaign: to telephone speeches to towns she could not visit in person.

They left Fort Worth in a motorcade to Dallas for one of the most memorable days of the campaign. It was also a turning point of the campaign in Texas for the Kennedy-Johnson ticket—less than a week before the election.

When they arrived in Dallas they went to the Baker Hotel to change clothes before going to a luncheon in the Adolphus Hotel across the street. A mob was gathered in the street and hotel lobby, but Lady Bird and Lyndon made their way through to the elevator and up to their suite. When they emerged to walk across the street to the Adolphus, where luncheon guests were awaiting them, they became engulfed in the mob, which they immediately recognized as an unfriendly one.

People were screaming and waving banners lettered with such words as "traitor," "Yankee," "civil rights," and something about "sold out the South." Lady Bird recalls that she felt "quite steely; that I just had to keep on walking and suppress all emotions and be just like Marie Antoinette in the tumbrel. But I must say that Lyndon was nine times steelier than I was. I think once he was in it he was determined to make the most of it."

She says she had no fear of violence but just pent-up anger and a feeling of how little these people knew about trying to represent 180 million people; how little they knew that every argument has many sides. "I was hurt, too," she added, "that these were the people we had been working for during the twelve years Lyndon was in the Senate, that we had answered their calls twenty-four hours of the day."

She showed none of these feelings, however. They moved an inch at a time through the banner-waving mob, many of whom wore Republican buttons. One banner kept hitting her head. She calmly took out her comb and raked it through her hair, which had become tousled in the crush. She wore a grim, unbelieving smile that was matched by her husband's expression. At one point they both turned to face the mob, as if to address them. There was silence for a bare second, then someone uttered an ugly shout. Lady Bird and the Senator turned around and pushed on into the ballroom. He placed his hands on her shoulders and whispered, "Don't say anything."

"It was a sad thing," she said later that day. "But I try to look for something constructive in it. I hope every good Democratic friend will be moved because of this to go home and get ten more friends to go out and vote Democratic." Maybe they did, because the Kennedy-Johnson ticket with the help of Lady Bird carried Texas to win the election.

Lady Bird Johnson remembers that campaign as an "era of cold hotcakes and early sunrises." It was also a time for reunions with kinfolks throughout the country. A high point of her campaigning was the whistle-stop train trip through Alabama, when some twenty-five cousins showed up at the station on one stop to wish her well. There were kinfolks in other states too, and she kept a "kinfolks" file to keep up with them all. In Alabama, a supporter gave her a rabbit's foot for good luck and she carried it with her the rest of the time during the campaign.

Her husband accompanied her on the train trip from Virginia to Alabama. "The people were pleased to death," recalls Mrs. Hale Boggs, wife of the House Minority Whip from Louisiana, who "advanced" the whistle-stop trip. "They said it was the first time anyone on a national ticket had paid any attention to them, and Mr. Johnson had brought his wife with him also. Mrs. Johnson is so multi-talented and does so many things well that I used to worry for fear a single image would not emerge on the brief appearances. But her genuine goodness came through, and that was best of all."

In Charlottesville, Virginia, someone gave Mrs. Johnson a gavel made from a tree on the lawn of Monticello, and she promised: "That's going on a foremost shelf at the LBJ Ranch because Thomas Jefferson is my favorite founding father, not to mention the fact that my father, grandfather, brother and a nephew are named after him. They are all Thomas Jefferson Taylor."

At their stop in Gaffney, South Carolina, Mrs. Johnson stole the show from her husband when she looked over the crowd of five hundred—many of them school children—and exclaimed: "I believe school has let out, for I don't believe this many would play hookey."

As she spoke in Atlanta, a sign above her proclaimed: "Mrs. LBJ is here today, Mr. LBJ is on his way." High overhead, a plane flew back and forth with the words "We love Lady Bird" on a streamer. She looked at it, turned to the audience and said a little breathlessly into the microphone, "Nothing like this has ever happened to me before. I can tell you I am powerful proud."

She held a press conference in the office of the governor, then went to the 125-year-old farm of Senator Herman

Talmadge at Lovejoy for a seated dinner with a hundred and twenty-five key Georgia politicians. That was a good sign of victory for the ticket.

New Orleans paid her and the vice-presidential candidate the highest honor possible in that city—it staged a Mardi Gras motorcade parade out of season. In New Orleans, Lady Bird found some of the local leaders a little miffed at her husband's quick change of plans, and in her own sweet way she smoothed things out. Mr. Johnson had not planned to remain in New Orleans with his entourage; therefore, no hotel space had been reserved. At the last minute he decided he would stay overnight. Although two big conventions were going on, local Democratic leaders persuaded hotel officials to clear a block of rooms for Mr. Johnson and his party. Then he decided not to stay but to go on as originally planned. The leaders who had pulled the almost impossible feat of getting hotel space, not knowing Lady Bird was in the room, grumbled: "Why can't he make up his mind?" She looked up and shouted a firm "*Amen.*" Everyone laughed and there were no more hard feelings.

The biggest thrill of the campaign, she has said, was "going through the small towns of the South on the whistle-stop tour, and as the train pulled out, seeing the people wave to us. I still get a catch in my throat when I think of those things. Sometimes I would feel the crowd was as large as the whole population of the town."

Lady Bird never complained of being tired but worried about her husband's fatigue and tried to take as much of the load from his shoulders as possible. In New York he had a speech scheduled for television but was weary from a hard day. So she volunteered to be his stand-in. In Texas she sprained her ankle but stood in line three hours in Houston to shake hands and have a word with several hundred voters. That night her husband telephoned from Washington. Instead of telling him about her painful, swollen ankle, she detailed the fever of the campaign, the size and mood of the crowd, and relayed messages from local workers. Then she said, "Now, darling, let's talk about you . . ."

On another campaign trip her airplane skidded off a landing strip in a heavy fog. As the plane finally stopped, she said gaily to the frightened women aboard, "Well, chums, it's over!"

Lady Bird learned politics from her husband in a long steady climb up the political ladder with him, and she came close to being as good as he at sizing up a crowd and telling them what they wanted to hear. She never used empty sentences, mere platitudes, but always said something quotable. At first she wanted to practice in front of her aide, Elizabeth Carpenter, before each public appearance, and she wanted Liz near enough to touch while the speech or interview went on, but after a while it all became spontaneous.

She gave each audience a message that was food for thought, and sure to win friends and votes. To an audience in Oakland County, Michigan, she confessed: "When I was invited here someone warned me, 'With your southern accent, you'd better take along a translator.' But I'm quite sure that Democrats talk the same language no matter where they are. Variations in speech and region and religion do not mean variations in goals. All our thoughts are united to this twofold purpose: to make the country a better place for all to live for all its people, and to make the world a better place to live because of our country."

She told an audience in Alexandria that Virginia holds a high place in her affection and she has many pleasant memories of taking her mother-in-law over the countryside in search of ancestors and antiques. She often amused her audience with campaign memories: Lyndon on a palomino horse in Albuquerque, New Mexico, in his best business suit, getting off and finding the knee split, then making a scurry for needle and thread to mend it before a television appearance . . . a bean feed in Palestine, Indiana, right on the banks of the Wabash . . .

Lady Bird's contributions to the campaign were manifold. She served as a crowd barometer or weather vane, as they sat on the platforms, and she kept her husband informed with whispered comments in his ear or penciled notes slipped into his hand. Sometimes she made suggestions for his speeches, or nudged his memory about saying things she knew certain audiences would be pleased to hear.

Much of their travel was on the Johnson chartered plane —a jet-prop Electra dubbed *The LBJ Victory Special.* For sentimental reasons he named it *Swoose II* (a combination of swan and goose) after the plane he rode on missions in the Pacific during World War II when he was a Navy officer.

President Johnson respects his wife's political judgment more than anyone's. After each stop on their campaign travels he would return to the plane, take a front-row seat beside her, affectionately take her arm or hand and ask, "Well, how did it go?" or "Whom did you see?" It was plain they were in this together and shared everything.

The Johnsons were in Texas on election day and heard the returns in Austin. As they waited nervously to learn if their efforts had been successful, Lady Bird composed two speeches: one to be read to the nation on television if the Kennedy-Johnson ticket won; the other in case the Republican ticket of Richard Nixon and Henry Cabot Lodge won. She was watching television in the early hours of the morning after election day and saw Pat Nixon break into tears as her husband conceded his defeat to a nation-wide television audience. Mrs. Johnson's heart went out to this slim woman on the other side who had also campaigned valiantly for her husband. "I wish I could say something that would help her," Lady Bird remarked almost to herself.

Then she turned to the "victory" speech she had prepared and began revising it to include a message aimed especially for Mrs. Nixon but not mentioning her by name. It was: "And to the other two couples who were our opponents, I would like to extend our best wishes. I am sure they know, as we do, that it is a high privilege to be one of the four couples to appear before one hundred and eighty million American people, asking for the top job."

She spent her first few days as Second Lady-elect at the LBJ Ranch going through telegrams and messages several feet high "absorbing all the kindness and jotting down replies," she recalls. En route back to Washington she stopped off in Dallas for some after-Christmas shopping at Neiman-Marcus and began selecting her wardrobe for the inaugural on January 20.

Lady Bird had witnessed many presidential inaugurals in Washington before she watched her husband take the oath as Vice-President and Senator Kennedy take the oath of President on that snowy January 20, 1961, on the steps of the Capitol. But never before had the ceremony been so thrilling. Weeks of hurried preparations had gone into the event to make everything as perfect as possible, but at the last minute the weather played havoc with the well-laid plans. Nearly ten inches of snow were dumped on the city the day before the inauguration. Every hotel and rooming house in the city was filled. By plane, train, bus and private automobile more were "coming down to Washington" to see President Kennedy and Vice-President Johnson.

Lady Bird had invited more than a dozen of her own family and friends from out of town: her brother, Antonio J. Taylor from New Mexico; Susan Taylor from Marshall, Texas, teen-age daughter of her other brother, Thomas Jefferson Taylor, who had died two years earlier; elderly aunts from Alabama and several cousins; her life-long friends from Karnack, Hugh and Dorris Powell, and many more. And there were many from Lyndon's family on hand, plus old-time friends such as Miss Kate Loney, his first teacher, who flew in from California; his favorite professor, H. H. Green, who taught him government at Southwest Texas State Teachers College in San Marcos; men who worked with him at NYA; and Bishop McKinstry, who had reluctantly married them in 1934.

Although she was busy going to all the events, Lady Bird still found time to take care of the many little details. She found places for her kinfolks and guests to stay; she bought a ball gown for a young guest who didn't have one; she scurried around and found dates for some of her daughters' girl friends when the boys they had invited could not make it because of the snow.

The proudest moment of all was when Lyndon—tall, stern and serious—took the oath as Vice-President. With his hand on his mother's Bible, he repeated the words after Speaker of the House Sam Rayburn. Lady Bird termed his new position "swapping a vote for a gavel in the Senate" but she was happy for him. After the ceremony, he breathed a kiss on her forehead that expressed more than words between them.

Lady Bird bore no bitterness whatever that her husband was not in the number one spot on the ticket in that election, but when she accompanied him to the Democratic National Convention in Los Angeles that July she had hopes that he might be. Lyndon Baines Johnson, the most dynamic majority leader the Senate had known in this century, if not in all history, announced his candidacy for the Democratic presidential nomination at a press conference on July 5, 1960, in the auditorium of the Senate Office Building. It was packed with reporters and photographers, who were awaiting confirmation of his anticipated candidacy. Mrs. Johnson was not there, however.

She was at the bedside of her eighty-five-year-old father in a hospital in Marshall, Texas. A television set had been brought into the room so she could see and hear her husband make his announcement. "It was a considerable pulling of the heartstrings to have to hear it from a distance but if I had not come here, and there had been no other chance for me to talk with my father, I would never have forgiven myself," she said. Her father died shortly thereafter. Lady Bird said she thought her husband's announcement speech was "very good. It was fine, strong and thrilling. I am very satisfied with his speech and what he did." She added that she thought he had a strong chance of winning. A couple of years later she revealed that he was not prepared to become a serious candidate at that time. She said that anyone who knew Lyndon at all would have known that had he really yearned for the Presidency at that time, he would have been working for it two years ahead of time instead of belatedly, half-heartedly, and acting as if he had one hand tied behind his back.

"He couldn't work for it and be majority leader, simply because there are only twenty-four hours in a day, and if you are a majority leader, that is absolutely a full-time thing. And he wanted to be majority leader and he wanted to do a good job at that, and he wasn't wanting to aim at the Presidency," she said. "But on the other hand, he is very subject to love, trust and belief in people that he is close to. The two closest men in the world to him were Sam Rayburn and John Connally, and both of them were determined to pull him, if they had to haul him bucking and kicking, into the Presidency. So, very late in the day, and not very actively, he did get in. It just plain wasn't contemplated by me, at least, that the offer of the Vice-Presidency would ever come up."

Lady Bird sat in the gallery at Convention Hall in Los Angeles and listened as Speaker Sam Rayburn eloquently nominated her husband for the Presidency. Giving the seconding speech was Representative Daniel Inouye of Hawaii, first American of Japanese descent to serve in Congress; and Senator Thomas Dodd of Connecticut gave the third speech in behalf of the tall Texan. Lady Bird was proud of her husband as she heard the tributes and the wild applause that echoed agreement. When the votes were counted the Massachusetts Senator, John F. Kennedy, had 806, more than enough to receive the nomination. Lyndon Johnson had 409. As Lady Bird left the hall, a reporter in the corridor asked her, "Are you disappointed?" "I'm relieved," she said with a faint smile. Quickly her face sobered and she confessed, "That isn't true. I'm terribly disappointed. Lyndon would have made a noble President."

She returned to their room in the Biltmore Hotel, where she met Lyndon. He placed his hands on her shoulders in a half-embrace. They looked long and silently into each others' eyes. Her expression seemed to say all that was needed: "Well, dear, we have each other, and we have come a long way—but this isn't the end." There were no tears that night for them, nor for their disappointed supporters.

That night both of them slept really well for the first time in weeks. Lyndon was still sleeping the next morning when the telephone in their bedroom rang. "At first I had a mind to say, whoever it was, that he was sleeping and I didn't want to awaken him, but when he said it was Mr. Kennedy I felt that I certainly must and so I said, 'Just a minute,' and put Lyndon on. To the best of my knowledge, that is when they first began to talk about his taking it [the vice-presidential nomination]," Lady Bird recalls.

There was no immediate acceptance. There were many people to consult, but, Lady Bird says, "We had to make up our minds, which we were willing to do, in a very short time and more than sixty minutes' worth was happening in every hour, all pretty important and confusing, and I can't say just how long it was. It was not a spot he would have sought; he just had not thought about it, but the way it was put to him—that the Party needed him—struck a responsive chord." Explaining how they made the decision, Lady Bird adds: "You remember that you have been working in political life under the banner of the Democratic party for twenty-four years, or whatever it was, and have been the beneficiary of everything that they could do for you, and here comes a time when you could possibly be the deciding factor in whether the next administration would be Democratic or whether it would be Republican, regardless of the role you would play thereafter or the size of the job you would have thereafter."

She agreed that Lyndon should accept the spot, but there were other considerations too. He had suffered one heart attack in 1955 and was now back at work as hard as or harder than before and she did not know when he might get some rest as majority leader. Both recalled the long string of sleepless nights he had gone through during various crises in the Senate. This might be his chance to slow down and still be serving his country in an important capacity. Once the decision was made there was the job of convincing his supporters it was the right thing. He thrashed it out with one group including Senator Mike Mansfield of Montana, who had served as majority whip while he was majority leader. Lyndon Johnson turned to Mansfield and said, "Sometimes I know you did assignments you didn't want to do; now it is my time to take up the broom."

Diana MacArthur, Mrs. Johnson's niece who lives in Washington and is now Deputy Chief for West Africa in the Peace Corps, was also in the room that morning. "When he didn't get the presidential nomination," she says, "it was a blow, but no one shed a tear. When he was reduced to second spot the next day—we all felt that in accepting it he was giving up too much, and was so noble about it—that's when we really did cry. We felt as if he were stepping out of the driver's seat he occupied as majority leader, to take off his coat and pick up the broom."

Until Lyndon ran for the Senate in 1948, Lady Bird, who had provided the money for his first campaign in 1937, confined her participation to going along with him and saying "Howdy" at the barbecues. She knew that voters had a natural curiosity about the family of a candidate, and she gladly went along but did not project her own personality or opinions on the public. As a young congressman her husband was aware of her abilities, and as he labored over his early-day speeches, writing and rewriting until the moment of delivery, he profited many times by her well-chosen words, suggestions and phrases, inserted here and there as she read the drafts at his request. He still submits his speeches to her for her comments and suggestions.

During those years she worked quietly at handling small details that in effect built new political fences and mended broken ones for her husband. She went to the office regularly to read the outgoing mail and often added in longhand a postscript to persons she knew personally. When she heard or read in the Texas papers about honors awarded anyone, she called someone in her husband's office and dictated nice little notes from herself and Mr. Johnson. She left a standing request at the office that she be notified of constituents stopping in Washington so that she could have them come home to dinner with Mr. Johnson, or if a wife, daughter or mother came along, she could provide some special treat such as taking them to a luncheon or a tea, or on a privately conducted tour of Washington.

Lady Bird began to take an active role in his campaigns in 1941, after he lost his bid for the Senate. She went to his headquarters to take part in strategy meetings between Mr. Johnson and his campaign advisers, Alvin J. Wirtz and John Connally. Her opinion was requested and she always expressed herself well. More and more her husband called upon her to do things for him. He was proud of her and had confidence in her tact and wisdom. He wanted to let others see these sterling traits, and began to draw her more into his public life. It was not easy for Lady Bird to overcome her shyness and share his public life, but she did it on the theory that husband and wife are a team, and Mr. Johnson's goals were her goals. By the time her husband announced his candidacy for the Senate again in 1948, Lady Bird had become actively engaged in the battle. She helped set up a women's division and campaigned all over the state.

Much of her traveling was done by car—by her preference—as airplanes, besides frightening her, made her airsick. She was thinking, too, about her little girls in case a plane crashed, killing their mother. But finally the day came when she had to go from the Austin headquarters to the tip of Texas, and such a distance necessitated plane transportation. Mary Rather, who was then secretary to Mr. Johnson, recalls that "we were all fanning out in various directions over the state that Monday morning, and if any had had time, they would have felt sorry for Lady Bird as she took off through gray rainy skies in a very small plane with one pilot and one traveling companion, but enough courage and pride to face strangers and ask them to support her husband.

"It was in this campaign that Lady Bird and I left Houston by car together another morning and she suggested that we buy only five gallons of gasoline at a time so that we could stop more places to ask people to vote for Mr. Johnson," Mary recalls. "Just before we got to Madisonville, which was to be our third stop of the morning, Lady Bird said, 'You ask them this time, Mary. I don't believe I can do it again.' "

But she did, and before the election was over she could reach a town and go down one side of the street and up the other introducing herself and making an excellent impression in behalf of her husband.

Both Lady Bird and Lyndon felt sure he would come out either winning or be real close to the top in that primary, but instead he was horribly behind. It looked almost hopeless, but there was another chance: a second run-off primary. Lady Bird and Lyndon agreed there was only one thing to do: pick up and try real hard again, and if they lost, lose by 40,000 instead of 45,000 votes; or 38,000 instead of 40,000. "I wanted to narrow that margin just as much as I could and make just as much of a showing as I could for myself and for him and all those folks who had already shoveled so much love and sweat and time and money into it," she recalls.

She swung into action and organized what some of his opponents termed the "Johnson machine." But, she says, it was made up of the people he had worked with in NYA; the folks who went to school at Southwest Texas State Teachers College when he did; and some she had gone to school with at the University of Texas. This time she flew all over Texas, many times with him, to all the spots where he had been weakest in the first primary. Mrs. Max Brooks, of Austin, was state-wide chairman of women volunteers and made lists of clubwomen she knew over the state who might be friendly and help. People began to make requests for Lady Bird. She went from town to town, and a woman in each would have a little gathering for her.

Gone was the shyness she once felt when she would buy just five gallons of gasoline at a time in order to have an excuse to talk to more people. Just before election day, Lady Bird, her mother-in-law and her husband's three sisters divided up the Austin telephone directory and called every number urging the people to vote for Lyndon Johnson.

Two days before the election, she drove to San Antonio to participate in the final speech over a state-wide network. The car which she was driving turned over twice, bruising her considerably. She climbed out on the highway, hailed another car, deposited Marietta Brooks, who was with her, in a hospital, changed into a borrowed dress, and shook hands with two hundred women at a reception in a small-town stop on the way. Then she drove on to San Antonio that night and made her first state-wide broadcast, which brought her a flood of mail. Not until the election was over did she tell her husband of the accident and then she did it with humor. "All I could think of as we were turning over was I sure wished I'd voted absentee," she laughed.

The extra efforts she put into that campaign paid off. Her husband won by 87 votes. But because the margin was so narrow there was a series of contests for them and all sorts of legal battles, extending from August right up to the time he was sworn in in January. What they went through during those months, Lady Bird says, must have been similar to what goes on in a concentration camp where there is prolonged questioning or prolonged tension. "But the nicest thing about it for me," she added proudly, "was the fact that I would often see Lyndon being the calmest one of a group of very capable, tough, hard men—all the lawyers who were working with him and advising him. I was just glad to see that he could be—and the times required it—so calm and level-headed."

. . .

Lady Bird came into her own as a campaigner and speech maker in 1960, but she did not stop campaigning after her husband became Vice-President. In the 1962 elections she started out again and was virtually a one-woman show as she campaigned alone. And three weeks before she became First Lady she opened the 1964 campaign for the Democratic party on the distaff side in Boston where she spoke at the State Democratic Committee to thank the women who played a big part in raising $600,-000 at a dinner for President Kennedy.

From Massachusetts she went to Vermont, returning home on Saturday to repack her bags and take off on Sunday for California, where she spoke in Los Angeles and San Francisco before Democratic women's groups. With this start, voters can look for this petite, forceful campaigner on the political trails this year, speaking for her husband and other Democratic candidates.

[VIII]

Hostess to Dignitaries and a Camel Driver

Long before she moved into the White House, Lady Bird Johnson was a leading hostess. She has a friendly flair for entertaining that makes every guest enjoy the occasion, whether it is a barbecue on the banks of the Pedernales River at the LBJ Ranch, an informal dinner at The Elms, or a state dinner at the White House. Her party guest lists are studded with stars in various fields of endeavor, and stars from the theatrical and musical world are on the entertainment program. Her philosophy for a successful party is a simple one: enjoy the people and let them enjoy themselves. And it works wonderfully well for her, whether she is entertaining a world leader or a few constituents from back home in Texas.

One secret of her success as a party giver is her ability

to mix the stars with those who watch them shine, in a manner that makes everyone happy. One government clerk put it well after an evening at a Johnson party. He said, "Lady Bird made me feel as important as the Chief Justice when she introduced me to him." Before he became President, her husband said, "I am proud of her as a hostess and of the fact that so many of the leading people of our time have been in our home on short notice—like Mr. Sam Rayburn, Jimmy Byrnes [former Secretary of State], Mr. Truman and former Chief Justice Fred Vinson." He added: "Fred Vinson once told me, 'I don't care what other engagement I have, if Lady Bird invites me, I'm coming.' " That is the attitude of most of the people who get an invitation from Lady Bird Johnson and her husband.

The first state dinner President and Mrs. Johnson gave at the White House was in honor of Italy's President Antonio Segni and Mrs. Segni, and it was a huge success. So was the first dinner party she gave after coming to Washington in 1934 as the twenty-one-year-old bride of a twenty-six-year-old congressional secretary. But aside from the fact that both dinners were successful, there was little similarity.

For her first dinner party as a bride, Lady Bird herself prepared everything from start to finish and washed the dishes afterward. At the White House she had the final word on every detail but a highly skilled, experienced staff carried out her decisions, made suggestions, and followed through on every detail.

Lady Bird did not know how to cook when she married and came to Washington to live, but she bought a good cookbook and learned. Her first dinner party was in the tiny one-bedroom apartment she and her husband had on Kalorama Road and the guests ate at a table in the living room. Guests at that dinner were the Maury Mavericks, old friends of Lyndon's from Texas. Maverick was a great talker, later became the colorful, much-quoted liberal congressman from Texas who won national fame as coiner of the word "gobbledegook" to describe government jargon during World War II. He was such a delightful raconteur and keen observer of current events that Lady Bird did not want to miss a word of the conversation, so she planned a menu that could be prepared in advance—baked ham and lemon pie.

There was no after-dinner entertainment except the political talk that Lyndon loved so well and which she was learning to enjoy also. It was an evening that went off perfectly for both couples, and one they long remembered. And that menu and dinner format was to be repeated many times in the following years when the guests were other good talkers who also happened to be political leaders.

In contrast, Mrs. Johnson's first state dinner at the White House as First Lady made social history in that it was followed by an unorthodox program of entertainment that for the first time combined Italian opera and American hootenanny at the Executive Mansion. The guest list itself, numbering one hundred and forty, was a masterful mixture of diplomats and politicians, and to make everyone as comfortable as possible the invitations went out calling for "black-tie" instead of the usual "white-tie" dress for state dinners. (The new President, who dislikes getting dressed up in white tie and tails, plans to have most of his social functions "Black tie," with a capital B, meaning long dresses for the ladies and dinner jackets for the men.)

President and Mrs. Johnson welcomed the Italian President and Mrs. Segni on the North Portico in below-freezing temperature, then escorted them to the First Family's private quarters on the second floor. There they presented them gifts before lining up at the head of the stairs to begin the ceremonial march down the red carpeted steps as the Marine Band, playing in the foyer, struck up "Hail to the Chief." Downstairs, President and Mrs. Johnson and President and Mrs. Segni stood inside the door in the East Room and received the guests.

The Johnsons' gifts to the Italian President were a silver desk box engraved with outlines of the United States and Italy, separated by a quotation from Longfellow: "Italy remains to all the land of dreams and visions of delight"; a silver-framed photograph of the host, an art book, *Treasures from the National Gallery of Art*, bound in gold-tooled navy-blue leather; and a letter written in 1774 by Philip Mazzei, distinguished Italian physician, horticulturist and agent of Virginia in Europe during the American Revolution.

Gifts for Mrs. Segni were a sterling-silver compact, a crystal bud vase engraved with the Presidential seal and signature; and a red-leather-bound copy of *We the People —the Story of the United States Capitol.*

The dinner menu, which Mrs. Johnson personally selected from suggestions made by her social secretary, Bess Abell, White House chef René Verdon, and executive housekeeper Ann Lincoln, featured crabmeat Maryland, filet of beef, waffled potatoes, string beans amandine, endive and water-cress salad, Brie cheese, and mocha mousse.

Although snow covered the landscape around the White House there was a hint of spring in the elegant white-walled State Dining Room where three centerpieces of springlike flowers were spaced on the long head table seating twenty, and smaller arrangements of flowers were in the center of the twelve round tables spaced throughout the room.

Because there are not enough plates of one service to serve one hundred forty guests, Mrs. Johnson chose to use the china purchased for the White House during the administrations of two former Democratic Presidents, Harry S Truman and Franklin D. Roosevelt. After dinner the guests had coffee in the Red and Green rooms, then went to the East Room where dainty gold chairs were lined up in theater style, facing a portable stage at one end of the room. President and Mrs. Segni shared a front row with President and Mrs. Johnson. Everyone listened as Robert Merrill, baritone of the Metropolitan Opera, sang arias from *La Traviata*, and *The Barber of Seville*. Then Broadway composer-producer Richard Adler introduced the New Christy Minstrels in a program of American folk songs which, he told the Italian guests, are as "indigenous to our culture as Neapolitan singing to the Italian culture." The seventy-two-year-old Italian President tapped his foot on the floor as he listened to the nine young people play their guitars and sing such songs as "Cotton Picker" and "Saints' Train," a hootenanny version of "When the Saints Go Marching In." Later he invited the group to visit Italy and sing their American folk songs there.

The President and Lady Bird want to share the full flavor of their life in the White House with the people who work for them, and a few minutes before the Segnis arrived at the mansion, she telephoned her husband's office and invited the girls who were still working there to come for the after-dinner program. They left their typewriters, rushed home to change into long dresses, and slipped into a back row in the East Room just as the program got under way. Also in the audience were a group of Italian newsmen traveling with their President. They had been invited by the thoughtful host.

Among the invited dinner guests were prominent Italian-Americans from all over the United States and many politically prominent Democrats. The guest list had been made up from names suggested by the State Department's protocol office, President and Mrs. Johnson's staff, and by the President and First Lady themselves. It was an interesting collection of judges, labor leaders, musicians, editors, lawyers, bankers, business executives and personal friends of the Johnsons. It was a preview of the widely diversified groups that would be represented at state functions given by the new President and First Lady.

Over the years in Washington Lady Bird Johnson's pattern of entertaining has expanded in proportion to her position and surroundings but the flavor is always the same —warm and friendly. As the wife of the Senate majority leader and living in an unpretentious eleven-room brick Colonial house on 30th Place in Washington, she entertained with buffet suppers most often. Guests were usually members of Congress (she knows most of them on a first-name basis), friends from Texas, and members of the Washington press corps who wrote about the Senate and its majority leader. Summertime parties were usually on the screened porch or outdoor terrace. In the winter, guests would line up and march around the table in the small dining room, fill their plates with barbecued chicken, baked ham and other delicacies turned out by the Johnsons' family cook, Zephyr Wright, then file down narrow steps to the basement recreation room where they ate at small, closely spaced tables.

After dinner, all returned to the wall-to-wall carpeted living room to listen to "The Leader," who told what he was trying to do in the Senate and how he hoped to accomplish it. He was always the center of the conversation and would often sit on the floor surrounded by the guests, who sometimes outnumbered the chairs in the room.

As the wife of impulsive Lyndon Johnson, once-shy Lady Bird learned to be hostess at a seated dinner for forty guests at a few hours' notice, and to entertain half a dozen couples after a few minutes' warning. An example of her patience occurred last Christmas when her hospitable husband invited a horde of newsmen to take a tour of the house at the LBJ Ranch just as Lady Bird was ready to sound the call for the family to sit down to their

Christmas dinner. As the turkey shriveled in its skin, the President took the newsmen through the large house. Some wondered aloud what the First Lady told her husband when the guests were gone, but those who know her best say she meant it when she acquiesced to his will with a sweet "As you say, darling," and postponed dinner until the tour was over. She never argues with or crosses him. She may disagree in a gentle manner, but in the end, if it makes him happy, she sees things his way.

Her husband was famous when he was a Senator and even when he was Vice-President for personally telephoning a few friends late in the afternoon and saying, "Grab that pretty wife of yours and come over here to dinner, and be here by seven o'clock." Such command invitations were rarely turned down. On these occasions Lady Bird was always ready to carry on as hostess and had everything as smoothly organized as if plans had been made weeks in advance.

When she moved to The Elms in 1961, Mrs. Johnson's entertaining took on larger proportions and a more formal pattern than in her former home. She gave a series of ladies' luncheons—three in a row for Senate wives—and initiated the practice of having speeches at social luncheons. She asked two or three Senate wives to stand and tell the entire luncheon audience something about her home state. It added flavor and enjoyment to the luncheons and enabled the ladies to get to know more about each other and the states they came from than they would have known just from talking to each other at the table.

Mrs. Johnson also gave luncheons for what she termed "women doers" or "lady activists" of this country. Usually the guest of honor was a foreign visitor. Once it was Indira Ghandi, daughter of India's Prime Minister Nehru. Another time it was Empress Farah of Iran; another time

Mrs. López Mateos, wife of the President of Mexico. These semiformal luncheons were sometimes held buffet style, sometimes seated, in the ornate dining room at The Elms.

Often Mrs. Johnson would lure stars from the television cameras and Broadway stage to perform. At her luncheon for Empress Farah, beautiful wife of the Shah of Iran, she introduced songbird Carol Lawrence as the star performer. Broadway musical star Karen Morrow and a college students' chorus entertained at the luncheon in honor of Mrs. Betancourt, wife of the President of Venezuela; and at the luncheon for Mrs. López Mateos, Carol Channing was there in her "Diamonds Are a Girl's Best Friend" role. Among the guests were former First Lady Mamie Eisenhower, who drove down from Gettysburg with her daughter-in-law, Barbara.

When Mrs. Johnson gave a luncheon in December, 1962, to honor the wives of Japanese Cabinet ministers visiting Washington, a Japanese cherry tree in the center of the circular driveway at The Elms blossomed out as if on cue to greet them. Lady Bird herself made them feel more at home with her greeting in Japanese: *Kon-ne-chew-ah*, or "Welcome, friends."

Lady Bird did not leave it to chance for the Japanese ladies to find out just who the distinguished American women were at the luncheon. In her introduction speech she said:

"An oriental philosopher whose words of wisdom have long accommodated the world for every occasion, once said, 'There are no greater pleasures than to greet friends from afar.' We in this country have been in total agreement since you ladies arrived. I am so glad . . . your schedule started you off where our forefathers and foremothers started—in Williamsburg, Virginia—and then brought you rapidly through two hundred years of history to see the styles and supermarkets of today's American women.

"Now I want you to hear something about the things we do. When I travel I like to meet the women doers in each nation. I thought you might like to visit with some of our own. And I am always so proud when we can show off such lady activists as Dr. Frances Kelsey, whose quiet steady watchdog activity is on food and drug consumption and means more than we can ever measure; Judge Marjorie Lawson, who strives to find constructive courtroom answers to juvenile problems; Dr. Nancy Roman, our chief 'lady stargazer' of the space program; Dr. Mildred O'Tenesek, who teaches political science and puts it into practice as Maryland's Democratic National Committee-woman; Mary Lasker, catalyst and sparkplug for medical research and discerning collector of the world's great art treasures. These and many more are here in this room."

With the assistance of her secretary, Bess Abell, and the Vice-President's executive assistant, Elizabeth Carpenter, Lady Bird introduced a guessing game for her guests to play in finding their seats at luncheons and their partners at dinner. At a luncheon she gave in honor of Mrs. Henry R. Labouisse, wife of the United States ambassador to Greece, guests arrived to find themselves cast in the role of Greek goddesses. Place cards on the table bore the names of goddesses rather than the guests themselves and each woman was handed a card describing the goddess she was to represent.

The "find your partner" game was played slightly differently at a dinner party the Vice-President and Mrs. Johnson gave in August, 1962, on the terrace at The Elms. Each of the fifty-four guests was given a gilt-edged card on which was written half of a political slogan or famous quotation of a prominent political figure. The men received the first half, the ladies the last half of the slogan, and the trick was to match them to find one's dinner partner. One slogan was former President Harry S Truman's admonition about politics: "If you can't stand the heat, stay out of the kitchen."

Lady Bird Johnson's father's store in Karnack, Texas, with the sign reading "T. J. Taylor, Dealer in Everything," which Lady Bird often mentions in her speeches around the world.

One of the earliest pictures of Claudia Taylor, held here by Alice Tittle, the nursemaid who gave her the nickname, Lady Bird.

The inscribed photograph Lyndon Johnson gave Lady Bird in 1934 before they became engaged.

Lady Bird's photograph for Lyndon, made about 1934.

Lyndon and Lady Bird Johnson on their honeymoon at Lake Xochimilco, Mexico, in November of 1934.

This attractive family group shows the Johnsons with Lynda Bird and Lucy Baines in 1948.

Home on the range, Lady Bird strikes a pensive pose against one of the centuries-old live oak trees on the LBJ Ranch grounds near Stonewall, Texas.

Senator and Mrs. Lyndon B. Johnson at the LBJ Ranch (1957). This corner is part of the original structure and well over a hundred years old.

Heart's home for the Johnsons is the ranch. This happy grouping of the family is on the fence, facing the Pedernales River, in front of the rambling stone and white frame house that has been in the family for more than a century.

Lyndon and Lady Bird Johnson, in typical ranch wear, inspect their white-faced Hereford from the fence at the LBJ Ranch.

Lady Bird and Lyndon Johnson ford the dam on the Pedernales River in their vintage roadster at the LBJ Ranch.

Lyndon and Lady Bird Johnson stand on the steps of the Capitol. This picture was taken following his return to the Senate after his heart attack in July, 1955.

Vice-President Johnson gets kissed on both cheeks by his daughters, Lucy Baines (left) and Lynda Bird (right).

With chapeau to please Mr. Jacob S. Potofsky and the hatmakers, the wife of the Vice-President sets out for a ladies' luncheon.

Mrs. Johnson shown here with Empress Farah of Iran. She was hostess to prominent women from around the world at her home as wife of the Vice-President.

Lady Bird at her desk at The Elms when she was Second Lady.

President Lyndon B. Johnson takes the oath of office as the Nation's 36th President from Federal Judge Sarah T. Hughes in Air Force Jet One *at Love Field, Dallas, Texas, on November 22, 1963. Mrs. Johnson is at his right; Mrs. John F. Kennedy at his left.*

(PHOTO: Cecil W. Stoughton)

President and Mrs. Lyndon B. Johnson (right) with Italian President and Mrs. Antonio Segni at the first state dinner the Johnsons gave at the White House on January 14, 1964.
(PHOTO: Cecil W. Stoughton)

Lady Bird, as a guide, explains the interior of the Capitol dome to Bashir Ahmad, in white trousers with knee-length black coat, the camel driver from Pakistan who visited the Vice-President at the LBJ Ranch, and then came on to Washington.

Lady Bird Johnson introduces Esther Peterson (left), Assistant Secretary of Labor and newly named assistant to the President on consumer affairs, at a tea for newspaper women in the yellow Oval Room upstairs at the White House. On the shelves in the background are Mrs. Johnson's Lowestoft china and Doughty birds. (PHOTO: *Abbie Rowe*)

Lady Bird Johnson consults with her family cook, Zephyr Wright, on a menu for one of her ladies' luncheons.

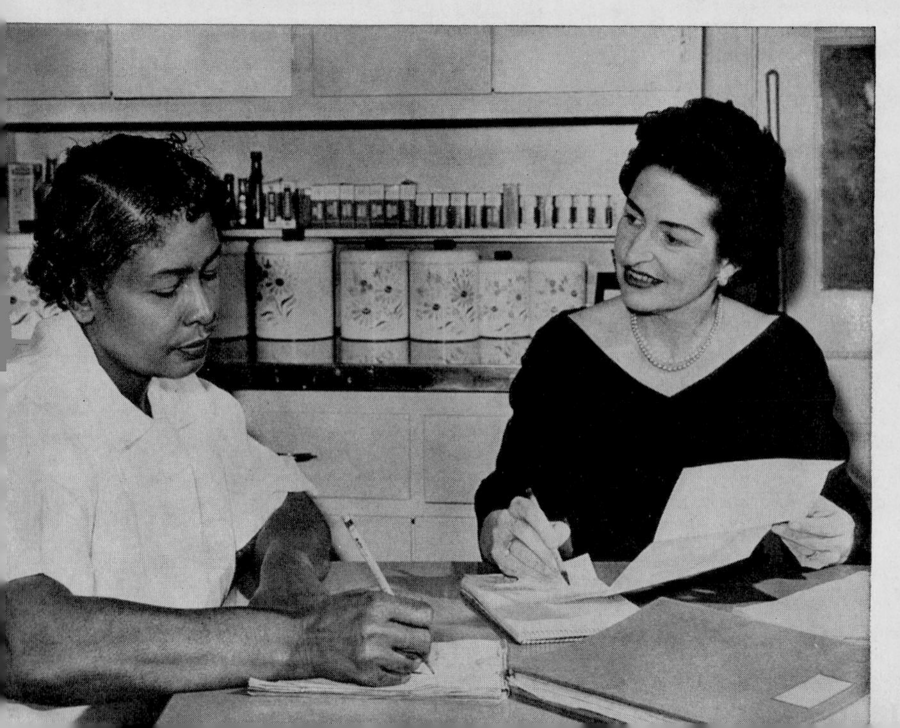

Lady Bird Johnson breaks ground in the rain for a new community library in St. Alban, West Virginia, to be built with the help of Federal funds.

President and Mrs. Johnson, Lynda Bird (left) and Lucy Baines in family portrait they gave to close friends and employees at Christmas, 1963.

Lady Bird Johnson makes a speech to children at D.C. General Hospital as she spreads cheer and Christmas gifts.

Guests at this dinner were invited to bring their swimming suits for a dip in the pool before dinner, and many of them did. It was unusual to see some of the hardest-working leaders and members of Congress relax as they sat around or dived into the pool, and to hear the gay banter that filled the air after a day of serious talk. Senator Gale McGee of Wyoming made straight for the water and began pushing newsman Leslie Carpenter in a floating chair. Majority Leader Mike Mansfield, watching from the sidelines, cracked: "I wish he would work that hard for me." But McGee had a quick comeback: "This is the first chance I've had to push the press around."

Guests dined on the terrace at seven candlelit tables decorated with arrangements of coral, yellow and white zinnias and marigolds. The food was typically Johnsonian: crabmeat casserole, cold salmon, fried chicken, corn on the cob, string bean and beet salad, peach and watermelon preserves, hot rolls, homemade fresh peach ice cream and angel food cake.

Lady Bird introduced the entertainment: Sally Jane Heit, Washington's comedienne-songstress who had the happy audience in gales of laughter with her songs spoofing the Kennedy Administration's physical fitness program, sung with appropriate calisthenics. This dinner was typical of many the Johnsons gave that summer.

The guest book the Johnsons kept at The Elms is bulging with pages signed by the hundreds who enjoyed their hospitality at the almost innumerable parties they gave. The names indicate visitors from all over the country. One evening the Johnsons entertained members of the Advisory Committee of the Peace Corps, a diverse group of business and professional people, and the guest performer was satirist Mark Russell; another night found the conductor of the Boston Symphony Orchestra, Erich

Leinsdorf, as guest of honor at an after-the-concert affair that brought together guests from the music world. Another evening the Vice-President and Mrs. Johnson gave a dinner dance in honor of Lindy Boggs, wife of House Majority Whip Hale Boggs, both long-time friends of the Johnsons'. There was another reception honoring Eleanor Roosevelt when she was named chairman of the President's Commission on the Status of Women, with all members of the commission as guests; and at the beginning of the Eighty-seventh Congress they gave a split-level reception on two succeeding nights to welcome the new members, Republicans as well as Democrats, and invited leaders of Congress from both sides of the aisle to be there to meet the newcomers.

As the wife of a Washington notable, Lady Bird was often asked to serve as hostess at parties outside her home, given by other people. Mrs. Kennedy called on her last year to serve as hostess at the annual spring luncheon the First Lady gives at the White House each year for wives of members of the Senate. Mrs. Kennedy and her staff planned the event, but Lady Bird stood in the Blue Room and greeted each of the ninety-seven guests.

As president of the Senate Ladies Red Cross Group she was presiding hostess at the annual luncheon it gave for Mrs. Kennedy in the old Supreme Court Chamber of the Capitol. At the luncheon in April of 1963, Mrs. Kennedy was absent due to her pregnancy, and Mrs. Johnson tried to make up for this disappointing absence by giving the Senate ladies an interesting lesson on the history of the Capitol. She told them about another luncheon held in the Senate Chamber exactly one hundred and two years ago from that very day.

"In the Senate that day sat, not the lawmakers, but Massachusetts' old Sixth Regiment, newly arrived in town—ragged, bloody and bedraggled, according to the descriptions," Mrs. Johnson told the Senate ladies in their starched white Red Cross uniforms. She continued: "That luncheon was given through the courtesy of a young Massachusetts schoolmarm. Her name is familiar to us—Clara Barton. She had arrived in Washington shortly before, full of Massachusetts vigor. Hearing that the regiment from her home town was arriving at Mr. Lincoln's call, she met the train, learned of their skirmish in Baltimore and saw their needs. The next morning she arrived in the Senate Chamber, where they were quartered, followed by five porters laden with boxes and baskets filled with food.

"Just what the menu was at that luncheon is not clear," Mrs. Johnson went on. "But Miss Barton's diary gives us some clues. Once she wrote, 'I made a washtub of codfish chowder which I treated in the old home way so that the Yankee soldiers cry when they taste it.'

"Another record tells: 'I have made a barrel of applesauce today and given out every spoonful of it with my own hands. I have cooked ten dozen eggs, made cracker toast, cornstarch blancmange, milk punch, arrowroot, washed hands and faces, put ice on hot heads, mustard on cold feet, written sick soldiers' letters home, stood beside three death beds.' But food was not the only fare," Mrs. Johnson added. "News was also scarce. When Miss Barton appeared in the Senate Chamber with the latest copy of the home-town paper, the Worcester *Daily Spy*, the soldiers quickly hoisted her to the top of the Vice-President's desk, where she read the account of the attack in Baltimore. Everyone listened for his own name—a tradition that seems to linger.

"And so, the mother of the American Red Cross received her training and inspiration in the Senate Chamber," she told the wives who work every Tuesday, sewing and rolling bandages for the Red Cross. As she finished, they felt a sense of pride at sharing in the work started by Miss Barton, and they felt sorry, too, that Jacqueline

Kennedy, student of history, had not been there to hear this story about a courageous woman from her husband's home state.

The entertaining Lady Bird Johnson enjoys most of all is done at the LBJ Ranch in Texas. Here Washington protocol gives way to Western friendliness, the keynote is informality, and the expansive space puts no limit on the number of guests she may invite. Once after addressing a Theta Sigma Phi convention in Austin, Mrs. Johnson, one-time student member of the journalistic sorority, invited the delegates to a brunch at the LBJ Ranch the following Sunday morning. Lynda Bird drove from Austin to assist her in entertaining the women and greeted them in typically Western dress: faded red dungarees, a red checked shirt, cowboy-type hat, and black suède loafers. The guests were called to breakfast in usual ranch style by the bong of a brass triangle. The meal was served buffet style and guests sat at tables on the tree-shaded lawn. On the menu were venison sausage, grits, mounds of fresh fruit, beaten biscuits and coffee. After eating, many of the women invaded the kitchen to get the recipe for the delicious biscuits.

On other occasions there might be three or four hundred guests at a barbecue on the banks of the Pedernales River, such as Lady Bird and the Vice-President gave at different times for Pakistan President Ayub Khan, for West German Chancellor Konrad Adenauer, and for the thirty delegates from the United Nations. Chancellor Adenauer came in the spring of 1961, when the land was carpeted with bluebonnets and the weather warm enough for entertaining beside the swimming pool. There was a Texas-style "state dinner" in his honor under the stars on a terrace beside the swimming pool which served as a watery stage that night for an exhibition by the crack University of Texas swimming team.

The whole state of Texas, it seemed, joined the Johnsons in putting on a Western welcome for President Ayub Khan of Pakistan when he arrived in the Lone Star State for a visit at the ranch. Vice-President and Mrs. Johnson shared in the welcome at Randolph Air Force Base where 45,000 Texans saw the red-carpet ceremonies. A spectacular 400-man color guard was on hand to do honors, and daring sky divers put on a thrilling air performance. When they reached the ranch, the Johnsons found the handsome, vigorous Pakistani President a man of their own kind: a skilled horseman, a hunter, and an agriculture expert who had risen to the top in politics and government in his country. Vice-President Johnson took him riding over the ranch to see the white-tailed deer grazing on the meadow grass, while Lady Bird supervised details for the dinner party given at small tables set up around the swimming pool.

The next afternoon there were some hundred guests at a barbecue on the banks of the Pedernales, where singer Eddy Arnold and a high school choral group from Houston provided the entertainment. Pakistani students attending Texas colleges were invited and it turned out that there were nearly a hundred of them.

"One of the most enjoyable evenings I have ever spent," Lady Bird recalls, "was taking the Pakistani ladies driving to see the deer which abound in those rolling hills. We soon found ourselves matching one another with tall tales and I confess they topped the Texans. We had some rattlesnake stories to tell, but nothing to equal their tales of boa constrictors in their country."

On another occasion, in April, the Vice-President and Mrs. Johnson rolled out the welcome mat at the LBJ Ranch for thirty delegates from the United Nations, who were given a bus tour of the ranch with Lady Bird as their guide. They returned to the banks of the Pedernales for an old-fashioned Texas barbecue where the Vice-President gave each a ten-gallon hat. The delegates were so impressed with Texas friendliness that Ceylon's ambassador to the United Nations, G. P. Malalasekera, suggested moving the United Nations from New York to Texas, where the delegates could "sleep better, think better, and perhaps accomplish more."

What this lavish entertainment of international visitors at their own expense means in terms of good will to the United States is immeasurable, but the impact is reflected in the letters the Johnsons received from their guests. Paying a special tribute to the way Lady Bird took the starch out of protocol, President Ayub Khan wrote to them:

> Dear Mr. Vice President and Lady Bird:
>
> I have not yet got over the tremendous hospitality, kindness, and friendship you showed me during my visit to your great country. May I say again how impressed I was with your sincerity and wisdom. I consider your President lucky to have a woman like you on his side. I also felt the same about Lady Bird. I at times felt sorry that she was put to so much inconvenience and hard work due to me which she bore with great fortitude.

Chancellor Adenauer wrote: "The days at your ranch, at Stonewall, in Fredericksburg, and in Austin will remain unforgettable. The great cordiality with which I was received moved me deeply. To me, this is a sign of the firm friendship which has grown up between our peoples, which, I believe, will survive all storms and dangers."

G. P. Malalasekera wrote: "The opportunity you provided to see Texas, the evidence we saw of your immense popularity among all classes of people, and the personal courtesy you extended to every visitor were always remarkable. They provided me with inspiration for my work."

Lady Bird Johnson and her husband were careful not

to show in a boastful way the many comforts, conveniences and luxuries Americans enjoy and particularly what they have at the ranch, but rather to show the progress and level of living that can be achieved in a relatively short time under a free, democratic form of government.

One of the most delightful visitors the Johnsons have ever entertained in their home and certainly the one whose visit made the most headlines around the world was Bashir Ahmad, a humble camel driver whom Mr. Johnson met on a dusty road in Pakistan on their 1961 trip to Asia. During the five-mile ride from the airport into the city of Karachi the Vice-President, much to the annoyance and against the advice of his State Department advisors, stopped the motorcade again and again to hop out and shake hands with the people lining the roads, waiting to see what he termed "the United States of America embodied in me."

Photographers had a field day when the tall Texan stepped out to shake hands with the smiling barefoot Bashir, who stood beside his camels. They talked for several minutes. The next morning a Pakistan newspaper, one that had not been too favorable in its comments about the United States, reported that the friendly American visitor had invited the humble camel driver to visit him in the United States! The story swept Southeast Asia like wildfire. Johnson returned to the United States to find that the papers here were also playing up the story of the invitation. At a speech a few days later in Washington before the Conference of Mayors, which had been active in the People-to-People program, he suggested they bring Bashir to the United States for a visit. They did. But it was not a publicity stunt and it was never expected to create the wide interest that it did. Yet, for days the story stayed on the front pages of newspapers throughout the world. Would Bashir come? Some said, yes, others doubted that he would.

Vice-President Johnson took time off from his duties in Washington to go to New York to meet Bashir, who arrived wearing shoes and dressed in a new *sherwani* (long coat) made especially for the trip. Bashir returned Johnson's handshake with a hug. Johnson welcomed Bashir in his native Urdu, but Bashir spoke through an interpreter. They flew together to Texas and spent a day touring the Johnson ranch on horseback. Newspaper reporters and photographers followed them everywhere. Asked if he would swap his camel for Johnson's dun quarter horse, Bashir replied, "It might be a fair trade." He said he paid $150 for his camel; Johnson's horse was valued at more than $400. But Mr. Johnson told him that when he returned to Pakistan he could stop driving a camel and drive a truck—the Ford Motor Company was giving him one. Mr. Johnson took Bashir to the Pedernales Rural Electric Cooperative and told him about the times when that region was poor—before water was harnessed to produce electricity. Bashir was taken to Dallas, and toured a supermarket where he kissed a three-year-old girl; he went to the Texas State Fair where he received his truck; then he visited the Truman Library in Missouri where the former President gave him a good-luck charm. Vice-President Johnson had arranged for him to visit the holy city of Mecca on his way home, an unexpected pearl in his growing string of new experiences. Indeed, Bashir the camel driver was already leading a charmed life.

Lady Bird Johnson had stayed in Texas, arranging the same hospitality for Bashir she had arranged for the President of his country when he was the visitor. Newspapers throughout the country day after day reported the exciting things Bashir was seeing and doing. These reports were causing a stampede for newspapers in his native

Pakistan, where the reaction to the visit was as if everyone in Southeast Asia had won the sweepstakes.

Mrs. Johnson flew back to Washington and became Bashir's guide for a tour of the nation's capital. She took him by limousine first to the Islamic Center Mosque, where he left his shoes (they hurt his feet but he wore them just the same) at the door and went inside to pray. Then they went to the National Archives and the Capitol. In the Senate, Bashir, impressed, declared: "This is the room where America is free. The sight of senators talking is a sure sign of freedom." After luncheon at the Pakistan Embassy, Bashir, who learned to write his name only after arriving in the United States, visited the Madison High School in Vienna, Virginia, where he shared his homespun wisdom with the students. He told them: "An education is the only thing no one can take away from you. Riches and wealth can go." He urged them to respect their parents, as children in Pakistan are required to do. He smiled constantly and gave off quotes which one reporter described as resembling at times small flares and at others glowing passages from *The Rubaiyat of Omar Khayyam.* To a woman reporter he said, "Each time you smile, petals fall out." He told Mrs. Johnson, mother of two daughters: "A girl in the family is like a spring among seasons."

Never had Lady Bird enjoyed a visitor more. "Bashir learned much from this country but he taught us much too," she said. "He taught us that you can be wise without being literate; that human dignity does not depend on books. He struck a responsive note in many Americans, and I am especially pleased to hear reports from Southeast Asia that every camel driver, every lowly man there feels closer to the United States because they visited it through Bashir's eyes. I was also touched that two public schools—the Russell High School in East Point, Georgia, and the James Madison High School in Vienna, Virginia

—completely unsolicited, started programs of sending supplies and contributions to Pakistan school children because of the smiling face and kindness of this one man. It was a lesson to me how much each individual, no matter what his walk of life, can contribute to the great reservoir of human understanding."

Letters still come in to the White House about Bashir the camel driver. Wherever the President and First Lady go, they are asked about him, and when they have guests at the White House, they do not talk about the kings, queens, presidents and premiers they have met in their world travels and to whom they have been host and hostess, but instead their guests want to hear first-hand the story of Bashir, the humble camel driver from Pakistan.

[IX]

Woman of the World

In 1928, when Lady Bird Johnson was a senior in high school in Marshall, Texas, the class prophet wrote a feature for the high school paper, *The Parrot*, under the heading "Hoo's Hoo in 1948." His (or her) prediction for Claudia Taylor was: "A second Halliburton poking her nose in the unknown places in Asia."

That prophet was wrong by only thirteen years. It was in 1961, not 1948, that Claudia Taylor, then known as Mrs. Lyndon B. Johnson, began her extensive world travels and made her first foray into Asia.

During the two years and ten months her husband was Vice-President she traveled more than 120,000 miles with him to thirty-three foreign countries. "My role," she said, "was to be an extra pair of eyes and ears for Lyndon . . .

and to give the people of the countries we visited a picture of what women are like in the United States and the role they play in the life of the country."

But she did more than that. She was a good-will ambassador who set out to build a personal friendship with the people as well as the leaders she met in each country. She wanted to know about the women of the countries and what they were doing. She learned the problems of each country and the solutions they were applying to them. She garnered ideas to bring back to her own land as possible solutions to local problems.

She was an organized traveler, and one with a mission. She carried a little black notebook every mile of the way, and at intervals during the day, or at night before retiring, she would jot down notes on her impressions in the shorthand she learned in college about whom she had met and what she had seen. She sent word ahead to each country that she wanted to meet the "women doers" of the nation. And she talked with reporters at each stop. Many of them were surprised at her humanitarian interests. They had expected her to be more interested in the social angle than the women themselves.

Yet, visiting other lands was something new to Mrs. Johnson then, because until her husband became Vice-President her travels abroad had been few and far between. "My introduction to foreign lands, like that of many people who grew up in rural America in the last fifty years, was through the Church's missionary circle and Richard Halliburton," she recalls. "Periodically the Church in my East Texas home town of Karnack collected a barrel of clothes or held a church supper to raise money for the 'heathen Chinese,' as they said in those days. And Mr. Halliburton put sand in our shoes as he wrote about the Taj Mahal by moonlight, or swimming in the Nile—exciting lands that lie somewhere beyond San Francisco. I could not help but think back on this as we visited the highly civilized society on Taiwan—with ninety-eight per cent of its children in school."

She returned from each trip with many new impressions and a montage of wonderful memories . . . about sleeping in palaces . . . dancing in the streets of Koropi, Greece, under the light of a new moon . . . seeing the Taj Mahal, not by moonlight, but opalescent and exquisite at high noon in 119° heat.

But these were not the memories that serious-minded Lady Bird cherished most on her return, nor were they the things she talked about for months afterward. Instead, she remembered the people—a whole world of people surging ahead, many of them "moving in the directions we can applaud." Often she would go from the cities to the farms "to get a picture of the country, which is often mirrored most clearly in the farm people."

Upon her return she said her head was a kaleidoscope: she had only to shake it and new pictures would appear. One of them was a new facet of her husband. On their 20,000-mile good-will trip to six Southeast Asian countries in May, 1961, her favorite picture was of "Lyndon standing on a platform in every country we visited and listening to the 'Star-Spangled Banner' played by a native band. He looked four inches taller and ever so stern as they played."

She remembers the trees and flowers of each country. "Exquisite orange trees full of blossoms greeted us first at Hawaii and kept appearing along the way; only when we got to Pakistan, with the countryside and climate not unlike Texas, did the lowly zinnia and petunia show up. Everywhere we were garlanded with the lovely flowers of the land. I recognized only a few. Familiar to me were the bougainvillaea, hibiscus and orchids—orchids everywhere. But many were exotic strangers—the lotus, the frangipani, the champi. We also went around the world with the mango. I thought the apple was the most universal fruit, but after this trip I am convinced it is the mango."

In Viet Nam she had tea at the presidential palace with the attractive and fragile-looking First Lady, Madame Nhu, sister-in-law of President Ngo Dinh Diem who was later captured and killed in a revolution against his regime. Madame Nhu, a controversial political force in the country, was surprised to see Mrs. Johnson and Jean Kennedy Smith, sister of President Kennedy, who with her husband, Stephen Smith, accompanied the Johnsons on this tour, shake hands with ordinary people. But Madame Nhu did not follow their example.

Crowds swarmed around the two American women as they went on their hand-shaking tour of Saigon—visiting the market place, handicraft centers, shopping districts, a museum, a language school and a hospital. Lady Bird and Jean met the nine women serving in the legislature there—one of whom was elected at the age of twenty-six. And Mrs. Johnson was surprised to learn that some of the lovely lotus-blossom ladies in tunic and white trousers they met in downtown Saigon were lawyers and doctors who spoke English fluently because they had taught themselves the language.

In Pakistan, the picture that comes into focus as she talks is a camel cart laden with an overflow load of Moslems, some in red robes and some in blue—and a tour through a civil hospital in which she saw "malnutrition to which I have never before been exposed . . . five-month-old babies weighing only five pounds"—a sight that left her heart heavy with sadness and compassion.

But it was gratifying to see, in this land so beset by the old problems of filth and poverty, the housing developments for Pakistan refugees. She described these houses as "a brand-new monument to the sand and the sea of which the country is made—sixteen thousand gleaming white housing units. Two rooms of cement, a tiny cubicle for a bath, a fireplace for cooking and a minute garden. The occupant pays one dollar and fifty cents a month per room and the government subsidizes two dollars. In twenty years the man owns his home. No one who has searched for inexpensive housing for migrant workers along the Texas borders can fail to salute a magnificant success story of man against his problems."

In the Philippines she toured Welfareville, the government-operated establishment for parentless or deserted children, a model orphanage inspired by a woman Cabinet officer. Here Mrs. Johnson laid the cornerstone of a new building for unwed mothers.

In "picture-postcard-pretty" Taiwan she was impressed with how hard the people work. They seem to cultivate every square inch of land, and they harvest three crops a year. And everywhere she found a tremendous accent on education which made her very happy. In Taipei Mrs. Johnson and Jean Kennedy Smith visited the headquarters of the Chinese Women's Anti-Aggression League, headed by Madame Chiang Kai-shek. Madame Kai-shek was there to welcome them, and both Mrs. Johnson and Mrs. Smith sat down at a sewing machine and ceremoniously sewed a few seams as a gesture of friendship.

Members of the League, who provided clothes for the army, and their children presented to Mrs. Johnson a white stole embroidered with a multicolored phoenix, and Mrs. Smith received a black stole embroidered with many-hued butterflies. Kindergarten children of the nursery for military dependents sponsored by the League then performed a classical style Peiping opera dance for the visitors.

In Thailand she visited the handicrafts centers and the cottage industries that give to the women in some of the remote villages the first coins they have ever earned as they market their wares to the tourists. Mrs. Johnson, a shrewd businesswoman, noted that "someone with real taste and commercial savvy could walk through those centers and find what is marketable and bring them home to us." But an even bigger idea formed in her mind as she saw them. Why not try this in reverse in the United States? Why not set up a national crafts center in Washington where the handicrafts, made part-time and piecemeal by women at home throughout the country, could be sold to the tourists in the nation's capital? It is an idea she has been keeping alive.

In India they discussed village development with Indira Gandhi, daughter of Prime Minister Nehru, and visited some of the old redeveloped villages. But Mrs. Johnson's most memorable impression was the night they dined in a palace built for the viceroys of England and now occupied by the Indian government. They dined off plates bearing Queen Victoria's picture, and there, in a mixture of old and new worlds—of Kipling and Gandhi—she heard words she will never forget.

They were spoken by the white-turbaned wise old Vice-President of India, who reminded them that no nation is "wholly right or righteous but that all of us have a long way to go." He reminded them also that "where danger is near, so also is salvation." Those comforting words Mrs. Johnson has shared with hundreds of women since then and she repeats them to herself in times of crisis.

On that six-country, 20,000-mile tour, Mrs. Johnson and the Vice-President practiced an unusual form of diplomacy which she called "global whistle-stopping," comparing it to her campaign travels. Perhaps it did not fit into the old pattern of diplomacy, she confided on her return, "but the old patterns have not produced all we wanted them to. And I am pleased to say that not a single hostile hand or eye was encountered."

Mrs. Johnson and the Vice-President returned from their trip in midmorning of May 24, and after the giant jet that had carried them the 20,000 miles landed at

Andrews Air Force Base, they were whisked by a Marine helicopter to the White House lawn, where they were personally welcomed by President Kennedy. He led them to the steps just outside his office and coaxed Mrs. Johnson to the microphones to "say a word" about her trip. She told the reporters and government officials gathered in the rose garden that she had been "people-seeing, not sightseeing."

While the Vice-President made his private report to President Kennedy, Mrs. Johnson went directly to the Women's National Democratic Club where she gave a report on her trip at a luncheon meeting of the Democratic Congressional Wives Forum. She told them: "I return convinced that it is important to meet and have the support of the people of a country as well as its leaders. Lyndon felt that while he learned from the leaders with whom he held lengthy conferences, he got a sense of what made up the country and what made it tick from the people on the street—from the camel drivers to the pedal cab pushers."

A few weeks earlier, in April, 1961, President Kennedy had sent Vice-President Johnson as his representative to the celebration of the independence of Senegal, a new nation in Africa, and Lady Bird accompanied him. It was the first visit for both to this burgeoning continent, and both were impressed with what they saw. On the plane returning home, Lady Bird wrote her impressions of that visit. This is the way she described it, in an article printed in the Washington *Post:*

> Africa is a many-splendored continent of bright color and contrast. My first glimpse of it came last week when we watched the celebration of a new nation. Senegal, which is the size of South Dakota, has a population comparable to Oklahoma.

The United States and 81 other countries joined the 2,500,000 Senegalese in celebrating its transition from a French colony to a republic.

How can one presume to know anything about a country after three days? Yet at its hour of independence, Senegal is so breath-takingly brilliant in the array of people, languages, costumes, and customs that one tries to absorb like a sponge. You overflow with impressions that you want to talk about.

The tall red-coated honor guard with shining sabers, a great palace reception with a tapestry of humanity as varied as the Moors and Malik, a walk through the fishing village of Kayar, and through the peanut-producing lands: these were the backdrops for the thrilling spectacle of Senegal.

To participate in the celebration and to see smiling faces and hear cheers along the crowded streets as the American flag fluttered on the front of our car made you realize that this new nation, jutting from the West Coast of Africa, is even closer to us than eight hours by jet.

While only 15 per cent of the people read or write, we heard their cheers of friendship in French or Wolof —"Kee-nee-dee," "Amer-i-ca," "Vice Pres-ee-dent." Once a Senegalese lady, baby tied to her back, smiled and called me "Yankee Lady!" Never as a Texan had I thought "Yankee Lady" would sound so good.

In six days we traveled 12,400 miles that led us not only to Senegal but to Geneva where disarmament negotiations were under way and to Paris for the 10th anniversary of SHAPE. We were back [in Washington] on Friday night in time to spin the wheel at the Cherry Blossom Festival.

Our introduction to Dakar, the glistening white coastal capital city, came at midnight. Meeting our plane was the tall slender white-robed Prime Minister Mamaduo Dia, whom we came to know as the capable right hand of President Senghor, the United States Ambassador and Mrs. Henry Villard, and the 25-member embassy staff.

So crowded was the city that the United States Delegation of Senator Thomas Kuchel and Mrs. Kuchel of California, Representative John Rooney and Mrs. Rooney of New York, and Special Ambassador Romeo Champagne, and others had to be quartered where beds could be found: in a French vessel anchored in the harbor, the hotel, or homes of embassy staff members.

There were African Presidents, Cabinet ministers, chiefs and traditional notables from sister nations. Many lesser folk had walked hundreds of miles from desert or bushlands and were at home on the sands along the beautiful beaches.

Lyndon and I were guests at the shining new United States Embassy residence which stands on a nub of Dakar. Its spectacular view is both toward the sea and the city. Nearby is the impressive Ministry of Justice, the Supreme Court of Senegal.

Everywhere the red, green and yellow flag of the republic flew, with its proud slogan: *Un Peuple—Un But—Un Foi* (One People—One Aim—One Faith). These flags sprinkled the parade, the festivals, the craft shows and receptions.

For three days, downtown Dakar did not sleep. Dancing in the streets went on all night to drums. There were impromptu early morning parades. Sometimes a Mairbou, as the Moslem religious leaders are called, would ride a donkey followed by drum-beating disciples who till his fields or go out and beg for him.

On two occasions I sat beside President Senghor. Though my French and his English made conversation cumbersome, he told me two things of special interest: first, in ten years he hopes all the Senegalese children I had seen in the market place early that morning would have some public education; and second, the women of

Africa are a growing force politically, and he approves.

The President is a poet of distinction and author of many volumes of poetry and essays. I also found him a gracious host to the guests from all over the world, whom he invited to a climactic reception in his beautiful palace.

Was there ever anything like it under the sun? A fashion writer would have gone crazy. Tuxedos and evening gowns were dull indeed among the great array of bright silver and gold *boubous*, the flowing outer garment worn by Africans, the feathered headdress of notables from the country, the turbans, and the stiffly starched white robes (with zippers).

Gold is worn by everyone, both poor and prosperous, as pendants, rings or chains. One five-year-old girl I met had her ears pierced in five places for gold earrings.

At the arts and crafts show, a typical African village with straw huts had been erected and gold-rubbing, boat-making, wood-carving was under way.

A fine strain of humor runs through the Senegalese. It was evident in the folklore dances which portrayed a wrestling match in which the wrestlers got mad at the referee.

So often in crowds, as in this country, the loudspeaker would announce a lost child, *un enfant perdu*, and soon the tearful tot would be held above the crowd and retrieved by grateful parents.

Since I grew up on a farm that sometimes raised peanuts, I wanted to see the land where this is done. Even Texas can't brag that its crop is bigger than that produced in Senegal with 750,000 tons each year. The harvest was over but we saw the lands and the copper buckets filled with peanuts.

We drove to a tiny fishing village where the day's take is laid on the beaches to dry. The chief came running through the streets to meet us and his welcome was warm, even through two translations: from Wolof to French to English.

In the capital and in the obscure grass-hutted villages alike, you find great pride in the bright new word "independence" and an aggressive accent on education.

But Senegal is symbolized clearest to me in the strange but fascinating baobab tree which stands sturdily all over the landscape and in the lives of the people. Its elephantine trunk is topped by tiny leafless branches. The vultures which hover over Africa often find it a favorite resting spot. Yet, it also produces an ingredient of cream of tartar and a gourd-like fruit called monkey bread, eaten by Africans where there is nothing better. The monkey-bread seeds are crushed into oil.

For centuries the baobab tree has been not only all of this but also a burial place for the most neglected and poorest of the Senegalese—the griots. They are the wandering players and minstrels, a caste feared and discriminated against by others. When they die, they are placed upright in the hollow trunk of the tree because they are considered unfit to be buried in the ground.

But challenge brings change. We were told that only a few weeks ago a griot was to be buried in the customary fashion to which another griot objected. A village fight broke out.

From Dakar, a high government official came to tell the people, "We are one nation now. The old customs must go."

In August of 1962 at President Kennedy's request the Vice-President, accompanied by both Lady Bird and their elder daughter, traveled to Lebanon, Iran, Turkey, Cyprus, Greece and Italy and back home again in seventeen days. It was a tightly packed schedule full of speeches for all three, because at every stop the Vice-President would proudly introduce his wife and daughter and ask them "to say something to the people."

En route Lady Bird and Lynda Bird had learned a few phrases of the language of each country and received heavy applause when they used them in their greeting. In Greece, Lynda Bird, who planned to major in history at the University of Texas, won an especially warm ovation. She told the crowd that when her father spoke first, she always felt like Alexander the Great, who feared his father would leave nothing for him to conquer.

Lady Bird found the exotic lands of the poets and prophets a mixture of ancient history and modern progress:

"In our country, anything that is two hundred years old is old. In Texas, anything that is a hundred years old is old. But I shall never forget the day I went to visit the excavation of the Temple of Artemis in Greece. The imprint of the chariot wheels on the old stone bridge, the bits of pottery and sculptured heads which were jutting out of the dirt, set me asking over and over, 'How old is it?' Finally my guide, the head of the Department of Antiquities in Greece, said with some amusement but also a touch of annoyance: 'Mrs. Johnson, everything here is B.C. except you and me!' "

She was intensely impressed with the span of time "that lies before you as you stand on the Acropolis and look down on the very rock where the Apostle Paul spoke to all the Athenians. Or, in Lebanon, to drive out from Beirut for two hours to Baalbek, the city where Cain fled after he slew Abel. Even in ancient times," she relates, "it was water resources that made Baalbek the cross-roads of the camel trails. If you are ever in that part of the world, I urge you to go to Baalbek, for it gives you the most thrilling sense of discovery. And before your eyes, you see the layers of history left by each of the conquerors who came, ruled, made their architectural mark, and then were overrun: Greeks, Romans, Arabs, Crusaders. Among the Roman ruins, over and over again were repeated the design of egg for life, an arrow for death, a rose for enjoyment. These glimpses into the long ago have two effects on you: it whets your appetite to go home and dig up your history books, your Bible, your geographies, and it gives you a new perspective of time."

She and the Vice-President were taken by the Shah of Iran to see the arid southwest corner of that country, which is flat, barren and brown like West Texas. The Shah told them about the great efforts his country is making to harness their ten-inch rainfall each year. With a loan from the World Bank and the engineering genius of an American firm, Iran is transforming that desert waste land into something bigger than TVA. She wondered as she viewed it then what it would look like in fifty years. Her mind flashed back to Texas: "What did we look like fifty years ago?"

"I think it is well for the American abroad to remember that it wasn't so long ago when we drew water from wells, when there were open sewers in some of our streets. Indeed, then we were an underdeveloped nation. Two ingredients, natural resources and the catalyst of enlightened leadership, spell the difference for us now," she says.

In between official talks with government leaders, state dinners, and tea, Lady Bird and her husband literally went "back to the farm" in Greece when they visited the American Farm School established in northern Greece fifty years ago by a Congregationalist missionary for Greek farm boys to learn how to develop a better breed of cattle, how to grow more and better crops, and how to be community leaders when they returned home. "We were given straw hats and loaded into a tractor-drawn wagon to drive through their barns and farmlands. I could not help thinking how jealous our ranch foreman back home would be to see those fat shiny hogs," Lady Bird recalls.

She was thrilled to see how one American's dream was touching so many lives, incomes and destinies at the school, which takes in two hundred boys each year for a four-year course, and also offers crash courses in irrigation, rural electrification and other necessary know-how to adult farmers. The students learn how to make use of what they have, and have even found a way to make a hot-water heater out of an oil drum and eighty-nine cents' worth of pipes and fittings.

She saw with interest the revolution of women in the Middle East, a revolution that has taken them from the veil to the vote—and in most cases, she learned, it was started and encouraged by male leaders who realized that their countries cannot develop their total potential with half the population behind the veil. "Yesterday, the woman of the Middle East was a storybook girl. We thought of her as veiled and mysterious, waiting for her prince to ride by. Today, she has ventured forth into the world of education, economics and politics," Lady Bird remarks. In each country she met women doctors, journalists, scientists, social workers, senators, deputies and judges at teas held by the wives at the United States embassies. And she found that each country offered a different phase of the transformation of women that is taking place—from Iran, where women still do not vote, to Italy, where they cast 52 per cent of the vote.

In Iran, she found, the big push is in education. Of the 12,000 students at the University of Teheran, over 2,000 are women. Just three years ago, less than 1,000 were women. She met the Persian counterpart to our own Bloomer Girls. Their organizations had such challenging titles as "the Association of Awakening Women" and "the New-Way Suffrage Association."

In Turkey, where women were given the vote and compulsory education by President Atatürk some forty years ago, women in public life and elective offices are not uncommon.

In Istanbul, Mrs. Johnson held a press conference where the ten women reporters sat on colorful satin cushions on the floor and wanted to know whether "American women consider themselves the dominant factor in home and public life." Replying from her own personal experience she said that women are partners, sharing the responsibilities in home and public life.

Their visit in each country had its social side too, and part of the assignment of their mission was to attend the state dinners and receptions where they met the leaders of the country. Two of the most enjoyable couples they met were the Shah of Iran and Queen Farah, and King Paul and Queen Frederika of Greece.

"In Iran, we stayed at the Marble Palace, which is their 'Blair House,' or guest house for state visitors, with palatial Persian gardens, fountains and marble rooms.

"In the ballroom, the walls as well as the ceiling were made of tiny pieces of mirror—one gigantic mosaic. When you walked in, you seemed to be inside a diamond.

"The Shah and the Queen were gracious hosts at the dinner they gave for us. There were twenty-four guests and, it seemed, twenty-four courses. As we went in to dinner the Shah took my arm and Lyndon went in with the Queen, but Lynda Bird had to fend for herself. I saw her searching madly for her proper place card, which proved to be futile since they were all written in Persian. Finally, by the process of elimination, she took the last chair and assumed it was the right one.

"The Shah not only spoke flawless English but was an excellent dinner partner, enlightened on all subjects. I found him vitally interested in the welfare of his country, and he is making a great personal effort to persuade the feudal landlords to democratize their holdings. He, himself, had already distributed among his people more than a hundred and twenty million dollars' worth of properties.

"The Queen lived up to her reputation for being one of the most beautiful women in the world. Having been educated at the Sorbonne in Paris, she is westernized in dress and in her open-hearted friendly manner. She has much more than a name-only interest in the royal charities which include orphanages, hospitals and schools. As a gift from our government, we had brought a therapeutic Whirlpool bath for the treatment of muscular illnesses. She quickly set about thinking of the place where it would do the most good.

"The dinner ended at eleven o'clock, but the Queen had arranged for a group of native dancers to perform for us in the reception hall. In lovely veils, they danced and read the poetry that tells the story of this exotic country."

Mrs. Johnson said their visit with the Greek King and Queen was a luncheon at their summer home on the island of Corfu. "The King and Queen and their frisky poodle met us at the door of a very comfortable but unpretentious summer house. Of course," she added, "that sunlit setting overlooking the blue Ionian Sea needs no adornment."

She described Queen Frederika as "one of the most vibrant people I have ever met. She filled us with facts and enthusiasm about Greece and its future. Even though she is of German descent, she is completely Grecian in thought and purpose. It is not unusual for her to set out in a jeep, perhaps with our American ambassador's wife, and tour the remote villages to see how they are getting along in all the endeavors the government has undertaken. In every way, she is a career queen—a mixture of Grace Kelly and Eleanor Roosevelt."

In Cyprus the Johnsons received the most colorful welcome. People heaped flowers, rose petals and branches of laurel all along their route to town. So enthusiastic was the welcome, and so many times did the Vice-President and Mrs. Johnson get out of the car to shake hands with the crowds that lined the road into Nicosia that they literally "walked most of the way" to this ancient biblical city that has been welcoming dignitaries, including St. Barnabas and St. Matthew, for two thousand years. It happened again in Ankara. Seventeen times was their car stopped in a five-mile ride that took three hours, and as the American Vice-President bounded out of the car along the way, he usually scooped up a local government official to go along with him to shake hands with the people.

"It was not the most painless way to travel," Mrs. Johnson said in telling about the trip, "but I think it says, better than a thousand words, what our country wants to say: that we welcome their friendship—that we want a base of understanding and communication with the twenty million people in Iran, the twenty-eight million people in Turkey, the eight million Greeks and so forth—not just with the government-at-the-top. For any personal discomfort I felt more than rewarded when a woman in a crowd pressed my hand and began speaking rapidly. The translator said, "She is saying, 'I've been waiting here in the sun for three hours. I wanted to see you. They once said you wouldn't stop, but I'm glad I stayed.' "

Italy was the final stop on the journey and Mrs. Johnson was thrilled at the booming, effervescent spirit she saw there. "Their burgeoning industrial muscles are busy marketing age-old artistry. If ever one needed proof of a wise program for a defeated nation, Italy is it," she noted. "With American help, their country has been lifted from the defeat and despair of World War II, and having been offered a helping hand, Italy was quick to lend one: it was the first country to send a medical relief plane to Iran after the recent earthquake."

In Rome she visited the Italian Baptist Orphanage and Rest Home for the Aged—and was greeted by the Texas flag. Here, too, as in other countries, Mrs. Johnson asked what the women were doing, and on learning that they make up 52 per cent of the vote, saluted "the success you are achieving in placing new importance on the franchise as well as the fashions of your country." Like every traveler to Rome, she tossed a coin in Trevi Fountain with the wish that she might return, gave a farewell speech on radio, and enplaned with her husband for the United States and home, their mission completed.

She brought back an interesting collection of mementos and gifts from the six countries: books on art and sculpture, engraved cigarette boxes, albums of photographs, autographed menus, and programs of events at which they were guests of honor—but none of these does she treasure so highly as the memory of the friendliness that was extended to them at every stop.

"Everywhere there was evidence of the people knowing and liking that flag and us," she recalls. And she was especially impressed by the "cheerful outpouring of friendship" in Iran, which has a "cheek-and-jowl relationship with Russia," and in Turkey, which is face-to-face with the Soviet Union along 1,400 miles.

Mrs. Johnson enjoyed a 15,000-mile trip to Scandinavia in September, 1963, with her husband and Lynda Bird, but was glad to get home. "Coming home is always the best part of traveling," she says, adding, "I feel as though I have just gotten up from one vast Scandinavian smörgåsbord of land, water and peoples. The centerpiece was the Baltic Sea, and both sea and land, wedded together, produced tables heavy with fish, dairy products and pastries.

"The sights," she added, "were as varied as the food. They offered snow-capped jagged mountains that rise high to the sky; fjords cut by glaciers that sink deep like icy fingers of the sea, reaching inward to the land; the plains of Denmark—abundant in dahlias and pigs; and in Iceland, hothouse farming by boiling water from geysers."

Some days it seemed as if she had walked through all

of Scandinavia. She wanted to see the farmland, and this necessitated walking into the fields, where she was impressed to learn that the soil had been cultivated for ten centuries. "We saw big farms and little farms," she said. "There were the cleanest pigs and pig pens I've ever seen; cattle scrubbed down daily; neat and tidy farm houses—and we tromped through the forests of Sweden and Finland, picking lingonberries."

In Sweden they were met by Prime Minister and Mrs. Erlander at Arlanda Airport and from there went to Stockholm by helicopter, flying over beautiful stretches of water, ships and forests. After they landed it seemed to them that the entire population was blond, with beautiful complexion. In the afternoon Mrs. Johnson went with Mrs. Erlander to visit two farms. The first was a modest family farm, housing three generations, where all the work was done by the man, his wife (who managed the dairy) and the grandfather. Then she visited a beautiful estate belonging to a couple of the nobility who lived in an old mansion showing remnants of great elegance. Several of the rooms had been charmingly restored, and here Mrs. Johnson had tea.

That night the Johnsons were honored at a dinner given by Prime Minister Erlander at the Royal Ministry of Foreign Affairs and Lady Bird found him a delightful conversationalist, who, incidentally, has been running the country for seventeen years. He told her about Stockholm a hundred years ago, when it was the dirtiest city in Europe with open sewers and a high mortality rate. It is now sparkling clean, and the people look healthy and handsome.

The next morning at Tullinge Airport, Mrs. Johnson saw a remarkable display of air power such as she had never seen. Sweden has one of the world's finest air forces and their *Draken* planes came roaring out of underground hangars and put on a ballet in the sky which was breathtaking. First, they flew incredibly fast in formation, then separated and passed one another very close to the ground at fantastic speeds in what appeared to be a hair-breadth miss.

The Johnsons flew to Sofiero, the summer residence of King Gustav and Queen Louise in southern Sweden. The King greeted them at the helicopter and led them the quarter mile through rain-soaked gardens of rose beds and banks of rhododendrons to the big, comfortable country house, a turreted, Gothic-style building of red brick. Queen Louise met them at the steps. Inside they found the summer residence comfortable but simple, bright with chintzes and pictures, and windows looking out on the Baltic sea. The King pointed across the Baltic to Denmark, a one-hour ferry ride away, where his daughter, Queen Ingrid, lives close to Hamlet's castle.

When she came home Mrs. Johnson listed the accomplishments of the trip to assess its value, just as she had done on the other trips. She came up with many pluses:

"It was the first time in a hundred and eighty years of national history that a Vice-President or President ever officially visited all or any of the five nations in northern Europe while he was in office, although all the Scandinavian countries have sent their prime ministers, kings or presidents to our country since 1960.

"The people of these nations showed much greater friendship to the United States than we ever anticipated. Within a hundred miles of the Soviet border, the crowds along the street stood day and night, ten deep, to cheer our American flag.

"They listened carefully and applauded when Lyndon, in country after country, spelled out our foreign policy in his best Johnson City language: that there is not one piece of territory in the world which the United States covets; that our foreign policy is based on the dignity of the individual, self-determination, freedom to be free.

"I do not think these points fell on deaf ears," Mrs. Johnson added. "Everywhere, in the farm homes and the industrial cooperatives, the conversation was about peace. I found that the Scandinavians, like the Americans, are greatly heartened by the nuclear test ban. The point Lyndon drove hard over and over to these leaders who are running the top of the world was that the test ban came about only because we had a NATO and a strong defense."

Mrs. Johnson proved that she has become as perceptive on the diplomatic level as on the political campaign circuit.

[X]

Master of Words

Lady Bird Johnson may well become the most widely quoted First Lady ever to occupy the White House. Not only does she make serious public speeches filled with quotable sentences that express the philosophy she shares with her husband (the type of speeches none of her predecessors, with the exception of Mrs. Franklin D. Roosevelt, made), but her casual conversation is filled with quaint expressions indigenous to the section of the country from which she comes.

People from other areas hearing these epigrammatical expressions for the first time from the mouth of the First Lady are quoting them as "Ladybirdisms" to show their identity with the wife of the President.

Using expressions she has grown up with, Lady Bird is apt to tell a departing guest, "Y'all come back soon, hear now!" Or, "I'll see you Saturday if the Lord be willin' and the creek don't rise." If she is preoccupied with a project, she may say, "I'm busy as a man killing rattlesnakes." Paying a compliment to the sisters of President Kennedy when she campaigned with them in 1960, she said, "I find myself, as we say down home, in mighty tall cotton." A person or group that acts impulsively or unwisely she would describe as the "type who would charge hell with a bucket of water." Someone who talks too much or too loudly is "noisier than a mule in a tin barn." Another expression, this one of disapproval, is: "I look forward to that as much as to a good case of cholera."

"She's a sturdy oak with magnolia blossoms all year long," she once said of her long-time friend Carrie Davis, wife of Congressman Clifford Davis from Memphis, Tennessee. She also described Carrie as a woman who "combines the wisdom of Dolly Madison, the warmth of Rachel Jackson, and the energy of Eleanor Roosevelt."

These picturesque phrases tumble out naturally as Lady Bird talks, and she speaks with an enthusiasm that conveys joy in all she does. This joy of living is one of the secrets of her vigor. Seeing the first snow fall of the season, she will exclaim, "Isn't it glorious? I'll know I am growing old when I no longer thrill to the first snow of the season."

Explaining her enthusiasm, she says, "I don't see how anyone could be less than enthusiastic and excited in the world we live in today. To be a part of all this in a small way, an observer with a seat close to the action front, is really exciting."

She expresses her own credos in a manner that is also original. "In this space age, passive citizenship is a luxury no one can afford," she says. She tackles each task willingly and explains: "Disliking what we are called upon to do is a peculiar sort of drain on one's energy."

. . .

Mrs. Johnson has a formal cultivated manner of speech also, the outcome of a ten-week course in public speaking she took in early 1959. As a result, her words today in platform addresses and in private conversations present metaphors instead of just facts. Lady Bird finds her inspirations close at hand. One of the last things she does each night before retiring is to pull back the curtains in her second-floor bedroom at the White House and look out at the Washington monument—tall, impressive and shining white in the floodlights. "If there is anything that will give you a sense of serenity and continuity, that is it," she declares.

She has read widely, from childhood down to the present, and often quotes from her favorite poets and authors. In one speech she quoted from the ancient Persian poet Saadi; in another from Robert Frost. She knows President Kennedy's inaugural address almost by heart and quotes from it frequently. She is equally well acquainted with her husband's State of the Union message delivered to Congress this year, in which he declared all-out war on poverty, and likes to quote from it as well.

She has an affinity for literature and says, "I'm a lover of good prose just as I'm a lover of the sunrise and good steaks—good prose is one of the joys of my life." She keeps a stack of books—most of them current, although she sometimes goes back to authors she missed in earlier years—on her bedside table for nighttime and early-morning reading. Wherever she goes—to the beauty shop or on a plane trip—she carries a large Mexican straw bag with a book or two inside to read during snatched moments. If she likes a book particularly well, she will buy half a dozen or more copies to send to sick friends.

An example of the modern woman emancipated from household drudgery, in her speeches Lady Bird elevates other women from the realm of kitchen and laundry to see broader horizons. She makes the vanity of fads and fashions seem insignificant as she challenges them in ringing words to dedicate their lives to making their community, their country and the world a better place not only for their own family, but for everyone else.

"American women are undergoing a great revolution in our lifetime," she says. "We have learned to master dishwashers, typewriters and voting machines with reasonable aplomb. We must now try to make our laws catch up with what has happened to us as we bounce in and out of the labor market and raise a family."

In her carefully chosen words—"and words are tools," she admonishes her audiences—she broadens the vista of women in, say, West Virginia, Texas, Michigan, California or Maryland to include the whole wide world. She tells them: "Americans have always attached particular value to the word 'neighbor.' While the spirit of neighborliness was important on the frontier because neighbors were so few, it is even more important now because our neighbors are so many.

"The need for human understanding and kindness grows with the crush of our cities. We must expand not only our brains and our wits to meet the oncoming crises of metropolitan living, but enlarge our hearts to include all the occupants.

"It is a rare American who can say that all of his ancestors were rich and privileged people. Too often we forget that much of our vitality as a nation stems from a bloodstream of 'the tired, the poor, the wretched refuse' washed upon our shores. So let us apply ourselves to this great human resource. Let us never deplete it through inattention," she urges.

"Our challenge," she continues, "is to seize the burdens of our generation and make them lighter for those who follow us. It is the spirit of Galilee we seek. I cannot help but think of that familiar quotation: 'Who brings his neighbor's bark to land, finds his own has reached the shore.' "

In her most widely praised speech she drew from her own narrow background in East Texas for an analogy to the world situation today. Her remarks made the front page of newspapers across the country and were praised in editorial comments. She made this speech at a dinner in Cleveland, where she received the Ballington and Maude Booth Award, given annually by the Volunteers of America for "outstanding service to the people of America." She told the audience of volunteers with a long record of good deeds:

"In traveling about the world with Lyndon, my thoughts have often turned to home and the small town in East Texas where I grew up. There was a funny old sign on my daddy's store: 'T. J. Taylor, Dealer in Everything.' It was pretty nearly true.

"I thought of it as Lyndon talked one day about air bases in Turkey, space exploration in Italy, a Peace Corps unit in Iran.

"Science and time and necessity—and I hope compassion—have propelled us, the United States, to be the general store for the world, dealers in everything. Most of all—merchants for a better way of life, I hope. I think the world is full of eager buyers who are thirsty for knowledge and hungry for freedom."

To prepare herself for the public-speaking role that seemed destined to be hers as wife of one of the world's outstanding leaders, Lady Bird went back to school at the age of forty-seven to learn speech organization, delivery and platform poise. She enrolled in a class sponsored by the Capital Speakers' Club with Hester Beall Provensen, who is on the speech faculty at the University of Maryland, as her teacher.

Shyness was one thing that made Mrs. Johnson tense when she stood up to address an audience, but she worked a great deal on overcoming this under the tutelage of Mrs. Provensen. Her nervousness made her talk faster, made her voice pitch higher, and the words came rolling out one after the other. She had to learn "reaction time"— to allow herself time for the words to form into complete thoughts before beginning another sentence or thought, her teacher said.

Lady Bird's first assignment was to introduce one of her classmates in a thirty-second statement. Her next assignment was to participate with another classmate in a presentation and acceptance ceremony. Her partner for this assignment was the wife of an official at the Australian embassy. An imaginary situation was dreamed up: Mrs. Johnson was traveling through Australia on a plane and her friend was meeting her at one stop to present her a gift. Before they left class that day Mrs. Johnson asked her partner to telephone and let her know what the imaginary gift was to be so that she could prepare an acceptance speech accordingly. When she telephoned, Mrs. Johnson was out of town and her housekeeper answered. The crisp-speaking Australian left the message that she was going to present Mrs. Johnson a pair of koala bears. The housekeeper, not knowing the circumstances, quickly composed an acceptance speech of her own. She said, "I don't know what she'll do with them. I look after the children and the dogs, but I can't take care of two koala bears!"

This incident became the topic for one of Mrs. Johnson's talks before the class because Mrs. Provensen urged her students to speak from personal experience and background. Even today, in her speeches around the world, Lady Bird adheres to this rule.

Mrs. Provensen also taught her organization of material and rated Mrs. Johnson "excellent" on this; she stressed the use of specific instances instead of general assertions by asking her students each time, "Have you 'peopled' your speech?"

Another of the criteria by which Mrs. Provensen judged the speeches was: "Are they informative and persuasive?" On this too Mrs. Johnson was good, the teacher said, "particularly at persuasive speeches, because she was quick at analyzing her audience and associating with them." Lady Bird learned brevity also, a point President Johnson, a former high school speech-and-debate teacher, practices too. He likes to tell the story that there are two kinds of speeches: the Mother Hubbard speech which, like the garment, covers everything but touches nothing; and the French bathing suit speech, which covers only the essential points.

In her class, Mrs. Johnson learned platform procedure, to wear not too startling a color in order to keep the audience focusing on the face. She learned also how to sit, with the knees together and slanted to one side—never crossed; and how to stand, with one foot slightly in front of the other. "This makes you look taller, more slender, and the hips look smaller," Mrs. Provensen said. So well did Lady Bird learn her lessons in platform posture that Mrs. Provensen clips her pictures from the newspapers now to use as "how to" illustrations for her present students.

Since her graduation from the course Mrs. Johnson has called on Mrs. Provensen several times for consultation and advice on organization and preparation of her speeches. Once, when the doctor had ordered her to bed to recuperate from a cold, Mrs. Johnson sat propped up with pillows, going over her speech with her former teacher. She composes her own speeches, sometimes turns them over to her press secretary and staff director Elizabeth Carpenter to go over and fill in or add finishing touches. But it always comes out with her own picturesque words, phrases and philosophy that stamp it indelibly "Lady Bird Johnson."

One of Lady Bird's favorite topics for speeches at social luncheons in Washington is the history of the old Supreme Court Chamber in the Capitol. It was in this room that the Senate also met for many years before its present chamber was completed, and Lady Bird knows its history well. She often gave luncheons for out-of-towners in the room and entertained them with stories about its history. At one luncheon given there by Senate wives in honor of the then First Lady, Jacqueline Kennedy, Mrs. Johnson told them the room was the scene of one of the first battles about fashions between men. In the brief speech she showed her skill at storytelling, and although many of the women had been in the room dozens of times, they sat in rapt attention as Lady Bird spoke. Moving quickly from one dramatic story about the room to another, she told them: "When the Supreme Court moved from Philadelphia to Washington and first organized in 1801, there was great division over how they should dress. Should they wear wigs in keeping with the British court? What about gowns?

"Thomas Jefferson, who was against needless official apparel—an early opponent of white-tie affairs, I'm sure—was opposed to the gown but even more against the monstrous wig. He said it 'makes the English judges look like rats peeping through bunches of oakum.' Alexander Hamilton was in favor of both wig and gown. Aaron Burr was for the English gown, but against the wig. The public enjoyed the debate and the decision was finally made. Justices would be gowned but not wigged."

She often quotes her husband in her speeches and one of her favorites is: "I think Lyndon summed up the challenge to the twentieth century well when he said the world has narrowed into a neighborhood before it has broadened into a brotherhood."

[XI]

Fashions with Presidential Approval

The secret to Lady Bird Johnson's chic elegance is her husband's good taste in fashion. Always immaculately groomed in uncluttered good taste, she has three hard and fast rules that guide her selection when she goes shopping for a new dress. They are: it must be functional and pretty, and it must please her husband. The latter point is most important of all. As a result, she has a wardrobe filled with dresses, suits, coats and hats that have received presidential approval. Many of them were personally selected by the President himself before he took office.

After twenty-nine years of marriage and husbandly help in selecting her clothes, the new First Lady knows pretty accurately what her husband likes and dislikes for her to wear. "Lyndon's preferences influence me a lot more than consideration for his job when I buy clothes. If I liked a giddy hat and I thought he would like it, I'd get it without regard to what the voters might think," she once confessed.

If perchance she should choose something he does not like, back it goes to the store, or into a recessed corner of her closet, to be worn only on occasions when he will not see her. This is particularly true of dresses with full skirts and shoes with low heels. He does not like either. So she saves her full skirts and low heels to wear at the LBJ Ranch when she is there alone and he is back in Washington.

As a result of her husband's interest in what she wears, Lady Bird has many more clothes than she might have otherwise. He surprises her with three or four new dresses a year. On a trip to New York to visit the United Nations, for example, when he was senator, or as Vice-President, he would whisk her into a fashionable little shop and buy her a dress impromptu. On a campaign trip to Detroit he took time out from hand-shaking to pop into a fashion shop and buy her a two-piece green silk dress. Once in Paris, while they walked down the street near their hotel, two dresses in a shop window caught his eye. He ushered her inside, bought not just one but both dresses on the spot. One of the most cherished dresses of her lifetime is a spreading white brocade hostess gown he bought her on a trip to Paris some time ago. "I guess I will treasure it all my life and mention it in my will," she said several years later, indicating how much it meant to her.

Lady Bird Johnson's wardrobe is filled with dresses and gowns that are souvenirs of her travels with her husband and evidence of his love and steadfast desire to spend his money buying things to make her happy and prettier.

The most important dress in her wardrobe today is one

he bought as a surprise for her two years ago from a newspaper advertisement. It is a dramatic black silk strapless evening dress, fitted at the waist, with a long, gracefully slim skirt. With it goes a long black silk stole. Her husband was reading the news columns in the paper when his eye strayed to an adjacent advertisement picturing the dress. He liked it, thought it would look well on his wife's petite, size 10 figure and ordered it without telling anyone. When it arrived Lady Bird found that it fitted perfectly. She calls it "my mail-order dress" and has worn it to two or three state dinners at the White House when her husband was Vice-President. Because it is a wonderful packer, she has taken it on several of her trips abroad and worn it at state dinners in other capitals. It still hangs in her closet, ready to wear at a moment's notice.

Fashion has never been the dominating factor in the new First Lady's life. "She wants to get dressed, look in the mirror, be satisfied with herself, and not have to worry or think about what she is wearing or how she looks," an aide has explained.

She does not patronize one designer, but shops them all and picks the designs she likes best. She is as interested in the seamstress at the sewing machine as she is in the designer, and shows a keen appreciation for their work in the garments she buys. She likes to go to the store and try on lots of things, then buy one or two of what she likes best. She may take them home "subject to my husband's approval."

As she tries on a new dress or suit she will ask herself, Will my black kid shoes go with this, or will I have to get a new pair of shoes and a new purse? Because she is always on a budget, if a particular dress means buying new accessories, she may select another dress that will go with what she has. She buys style and quality in accessories to make them last. Her shoes will last for years.

Long ago she gave up T-straps and fancy shoes for plain high-heeled pumps, buying the same style year after year in different colors or materials. She admits her narrow foot is hard to fit, and that is one reason she likes plain pumps. Also, they go well with everything. She goes in for colored shoes for evening and may have them dyed to match a particular dress.

Her biggest clothes problem since moving into the White House is that she cannot go quietly into a store now and look down the rack for what she wants. She is trying to find a solution rather than having designers send their line to the White House for her to choose from as some preceding First Ladies have done. Since becoming First Lady, she has been asking friends whose fashion judgment she values to go to the stores and select things to be sent to the White House for her approval. This, however, has not worked out quite satisfactorily because most of her friends whom she would tap for this favor lead such busy lives that she does not wish to encumber them with an additional duty for her. Once she went to New York and had two or three stores send specific items to her hotel suite for her to choose from. This may become her pattern for buying.

A cautious shopper who never buys on impulse, Mrs. Johnson plans her wardrobe in a businesslike manner, and thinks carefully how each item will clean, pack and travel before she buys. Each spring and fall she sets aside one day—though sometimes it runs into a day and a half—for taking stock of her wardrobe. She then buys her basic needs at regular prices in her favorite stores. She fills out her wardrobe at sales. She tries to get her clothes-buying out of the way as early as possible each season so that "shopping does not run or ruin my life."

For years it has been almost a ritual for her to go to

the after-Christmas sales at Neiman-Marcus in Dallas, where she opened her first charge account at the age of sixteen. At these sales she always rounds out her wardrobe with a suit or two, an afternoon dress and one for the evening.

Mrs. Johnson also buys at the after-Christmas sales in Washington stores, shopping not only in the big ones but also in several little stores in Georgetown and exclusive fashion shops on Connecticut Avenue. The dramatic white chiffon accordion-pleated Grecian-style evening dress she wore to the first state dinner she and President Johnson gave at the White House for Italy's President Antonio Segni in January was bought at an after-Christmas sale.

She did not go to the store for it, though. It was selected by a friend and sent to the White House for her approval. She did not give out the designer's name ("We did not even look for it," an aide says), but it was a becoming style with a deep V-neckline in front and back, sleeveless, with a black velvet ribbon catching the pleats at the waist. With it she wore a single strand of pearls that was a gift from her husband several years ago, and tiny pearl earrings.

Mrs. Johnson has a clothes budget and sticks by it. Unlike the federal budget, her clothes budget is a secret and still modest, although it has expanded considerably since she was a senator's wife. Then she bought a new suit each fall and spring, and a new evening or cocktail dress each season. Just before he became Vice-President she added a second cocktail dress each season to see her through her expanding social schedule. She kept on hand then, to meet her social and daily needs, two long good-looking evening dresses for state dinners (one dress was white satin with spaghetti straps and a deep-pink satin stole, the other a bright-red satin dress, both purchased at after-Christmas sales), two smart dark basic daytime frocks that could be worn to luncheons or, with the jacket removed, to the theater at night, and one or two of what she termed day-in-and-day-out dresses to wear to pick up the children at school and go to market.

Even today, with the many social, political and official demands for her appearance, Mrs. Johnson prefers a few good clothes that she can depend on to a wide variety in perishable fabrics or styles that soon become outmoded. As do so many well-dressed women, she will wear a dress or suit several seasons if she feels comfortable in it, likes it, and it is still in style. That is one reason she prefers classic designs to high style in her buying—she can wear what she likes longer. Evidence of the fact that her wardrobe is not overstocked was her reply when the Secretary of the Smithsonian Institution, Dr. Leonard Carmichael, asked her for a ball gown to add to the Smithsonian's exhibit of First Ladies' gowns. Mrs. Johnson said she could let him have one for the January opening of the new Museum of History and Technology but added, "I may have to borrow it back later to wear some more."

She still has and enjoys wearing the glamorous Persian-coral coupe de velour creation (styled by Roxanne for Samuel Winston) which was her inaugural ball gown. It is strapless (a style she and her husband like because it shows her well-shaped shoulders), with diagonal pleats cinching in the waist above a bell-shaped skirt. She has carried it on her world travels and worn it to several state dinners in other countries. Like the rest of her inaugural wardrobe, it came from Neiman-Marcus. For the symphony concert and inaugural gala that year, she wore an antique-green gown of silk damask, designed by Magda, with a full skirt that had a curved slit at the front hemline.

For the inaugural ceremony itself, she wore a Ben Zuckerman suit of parrot-green crisp silk-and-wool fabric with the jacket lined in silk tussah woven in pink, lilac and green horizontal stripes. A small hat of the same green fabric completed the costume. She liked the suit so well that she ordered a copy of it in brown and wore both suits so often that each lasted for only one year.

Mrs. Johnson can wear a coat for years and has a variety of good ones from which to choose in the winter. First and foremost is her full-length Autumn Haze mink coat which her husband gave to her in December of 1960 as a "combination wedding-anniversary, Christmas, and several-birthdays-yet-to-come" present. On their twenty-fifth wedding anniversary he gave her a white fox clutch cape. She has a mink stole also. In her wardrobe, too, is a good black cloth coat, a semifitted beige cloth coat, and a straight-line red coat that is several years old.

Unlike many wives in public life who keep a record of when they wear each dress, Mrs. Johnson does not waste time on such details. If she has a favorite dress, she wears it again and again, unmindful of the fact that many of the same people may see it or that it may be pictured in the newspapers repeatedly. One of her favorite dresses at the time she became First Lady was a deep-red wool knit fashioned along princess lines, with short sleeves and a short fitted jacket. She wore it when she cut the ribbon opening the YWCA's International Food Fair in Washington last November; she wore it again when she went to D.C. General Hospital just before Christmas to distribute gifts to patients in the children's wing; and she wore it in early January when she went to Scranton and Wilkes-Barre, Pennsylvania, to inspect what the Area Redevelopment Agency has done to provide jobs in that area of high unemployment. On each occasion she was photographed many times, and each time the pictures appeared in the newspapers. But it did not seem to matter to her.

She does not try to be exclusive in her clothes and does not mind meeting someone wearing an exact copy of her dress. One day she saw a picture in an Austin, Texas, newspaper of her close friend Nellie Connally and noticed that she was wearing a dress identical to one she herself had. She clipped out the picture and wrote on it, "We have dresses just alike. I love mine too!" and sent it to Mrs. Connally.

If Lady Bird buys a dress and likes it, she will get the same one in a different color. She genuinely likes color and so does her husband. His favorite color for her is salmon, and if he sees someone else wearing that color he may remark, "That is the color I want Lady Bird to wear." Her wardrobe is a contrast and balance between white, black and bright bold colors. "Black is almost inescapable; it is so dependable," she says. But she will choose color any time. Mrs. Johnson likes yellow (all shades), white and coral. (These colors show up not only in her wardrobe, but in her house, her flower arrangements and her garden. She likes tiger lilies in the garden and plants coral, yellow, and white zinnias together. The rose bushes she planted in the garden at The Elms were coral and white, and in the big stone planters on either side of the front steps at The Elms were geraniums that had coral and white blossoms.)

Most of her dresses and suits have slim skirts because her husband likes them this way. She deviates from this, however, in selecting dresses for campaigning and travel. She will choose a dress with flat box pleats that give a slim silhouette but also allow the necessary width for taking big steps getting in and out of planes and automobiles and climbing steps. In selecting her wardrobe for her travels abroad, she says, "I lean on the advice of knowledgeable friends, study the schedule and fashion news, and keep my fingers crossed."

For her suits she chooses a crisp firm fabric, steering away from the bulky weaves so popular today. The reason is that her husband says, "I don't like those horse-blanket suits," referring to the bulky fabrics. He is also dead set against what he calls "muley colors," his graphic description of the wide range of almost colorless grays and browns so strongly favored by some fashion designers.

Although she prefers not to wear a hat, and rarely wore one for years, she seldom goes out in the daytime now without a hat. The change started a couple of years ago when she sat next to Jacob S. Potofsky at a dinner party Secretary of Labor and Mrs. Arthur Goldberg gave for the Vice-President and Mrs. Johnson. Mr. Potofsky, president of the Amalgamated Clothing Workers of America, told her, "You ladies in public life don't realize that the way you dress affects the lives and incomes of many people. You don't wear hats and you are not doing a thing for the hat industry—it is going to rack and ruin." The next day, conscience-stricken, she went out and bought a new hat. She told a friend, "I am wearing this hat for Mr. Potofsky and the hat makers." Several times since then she has started out to a luncheon hatless. At the door she would remember, turn back and go upstairs, saying, "I must wear my hat for Mr. Potofsky."

Jewelry is mainly a sentimental matter with the new First Lady. She has several good pieces but wears them sparingly. She is almost never without a handsome gold bracelet on her left arm. It is actually a watch that was a Christmas present from her husband several years ago. "He teasingly calls it a 'blind woman's watch,' " she said recently, lifting the clasp to show a watch dial. The figures are extra large so she can read them without using her glasses. (She wears horn-rimmed glasses, with a string to hang them around her neck, when she reads.)

She has three good pearl necklaces, a short single strand, a triple strand, and a moderately long rope single strand. She also has an inexpensive single-strand pearl necklace to wear in the daytime, saving her good pearls for evening and formal wear. She rarely wears earrings, except a tiny pearl on each ear to match her necklace. She also has a charm bracelet that she wears on informal occasions, and several scatter pins to brighten a plain dress or costume.

For evenings at home Mrs. Johnson's number one choice of what to wear is a glamorous red hostess robe. She has had a series of them over the years—wore one particularly well-liked red satin robe for eight years, got another red one the Christmas before her husband became Vice-President, and for her birthday last year her husband gave her another very feminine-looking red wool hostess gown for their evenings before the fire at the White House.

Mrs. Johnson does not go in for Capri pants and slacks that are favored so strongly by many of today's young moderns for at-home wear. She occasionally wears silk slacks on Sunday afternoons and evenings at the LBJ Ranch. For riding around the ranch on horseback or in the electric cart, she puts on her beige jodhpurs or riding pants, but she prefers the feminine look of a short dress to slacks or shorts.

Her clothes get gentle care that makes them last longer. If she finds a rip or tear she follows through immediately with repairs. She practices the same thrift in cleaning her clothes that she does in buying them. Because cleaning is an expensive item, she has her clothes cleaned only when they need it, relies on spot-cleaning and careful pressings in-between. She has the help of Helen Williams in keeping her clothes wearable. Mrs. Williams, an attractive Negro woman from Texas who has been on the Johnsons' household staff for several years, traveled with Mrs. Johnson some of the time during the 1960 campaign.

. . .

Lady Bird Johnson gratefully accepts her husband's help in choosing her wardrobe, but does not have much to say in what he wears. He buys his own clothes: a dozen shirts at a time with his name, not just his initials, embroidered over the left-hand pocket. He will have a tailor make him two or more suits at the same time. Always sartorially smart, he sometimes goes in for flamboyant evening wear. He showed up on the Washington social scene one year in a handsome gray tuxedo—the only man so unconventionally dressed in the VIP audience.

Sometimes Lady Bird buys him a bathing suit or slacks as a present. He can count on her also to see that he has a bow tie, new belt or suspenders when needed. But it is Lyndon Johnson who picks the fashions for the LBJ family, and this includes his two daughters as well as his wife.

He started selecting his wife's clothes long before designer Anne Fogarty advised men, "If you adore her, adorn her." His obvious pleasure in choosing clothes for his wife and two daughters is really a tangible expression of his affection for them. "I think they are pretty, and I enjoy helping them to look as pretty as they deserve," he says. Lady Bird sees it as another facet of his passion for perfection. "Lyndon thinks you should take what the Good Lord gives you and make the most of it," she says. She shares this philosophy and is constantly engaged in a self-improvement program of her own. With self-discipline she whittled down her size 14 figure to a perfect size 10 and keeps it there, although it is difficult to do so, attending as many official dinners as she does. Her secret, she says, is "to take small servings. I know there will be many courses, so I have only to eat a little of each. I like to sample the typical foods of a country and this small-portion plan is perfect." At home she practices even stronger self-discipline, and does not reach for that second biscuit.

A couple of years ago she took a course in make-up from Eddie Senz in New York and learned how to apply cosmetics without that painted look, learned the trick of eye makeup to accentuate her brown eyes (her best feature) to give her face a softer, more sophisticated appearance. She had her hair cut short because Lyndon liked it that way; then when Jacqueline Kennedy became First Lady and the bouffant style swept the country, she switched to Mrs. Kennedy's French-born hairdresser, Jean Louis, who styled her hair away from her face, with no parting and with a bouffant, unfussy look. For permanent waves, which she gets about three times a year, she goes to the hairdresser she had all the years her husband was a senator. He is Norwegian-born Per Hellekjaer, who serves an exclusive Georgetown clientele that includes several Cabinet wives and socially prominent Washingtonians.

Although Mrs. Johnson is fifty-one years of age, there is almost no gray or white in her hair and she does not need a rinse to heighten the color. As First Lady her request for a hairdresser to come to the White House to take care of her hair would be promptly heeded, but she does not always ask for it. Since moving into the White House she has gone to the elegant Connecticut Avenue salon of Jean Louis, and also to Per's salon in Georgetown where the curtained booths give her so much privacy that the other clients never know she is there unless they see the Secret Service agent who keeps an eye on her booth from the waiting room.

Lady Bird gives her husband grateful credit for stimulating her interest in clothes and attributes it to his leadership qualities. "He always expects more of you—I mean, if you are someone he cares a great deal about—than you think you are really mentally or physically capable of putting out. And somehow that makes you try a little bit harder and makes you proceed a little more. It is really very stimulating. It is also very tiring.

"For example, he always expects me to look better than I do, which means that I have to make up in grooming and buying clothes and taking exercises for what doesn't come naturally. Sometimes I want to rebel against that, for I am somewhat reluctant about being so materialistic. But every now and then I see someone who is just my own age and I imagine that I look younger and act younger, and if I do, it is because I have done all the extra things to look and feel better."

She gives her husband credit also for helping her to develop in personality. "I was a much less gregarious person, much less interested in people, less outgoing or willing to make contact with others before I began to live with Lyndon. He has made me realize that it is more fun to have your life touch the lives of a lot of people, and let them know you like them. So, if there have been any growth and broadening in my relationships, if I have any more friends, I must give him a lot of credit for that too."

It is a generous wife, indeed, who gives her husband credit for her outward chic appearance and also for the warm friendliness she has toward other people. Lady Bird Johnson is that generous person.

[XII]

At the LBJ Ranch

Heart's home to Lyndon and Lady Bird Johnson is a sprawling 438-acre ranch deep in the heart of the Texas hill country where the welcome mat at the front door of the century-old ranch house reads: *All the World is Welcome Here.*

This statement is literally true, for four heads of state plus high ranking official representatives of more than half the countries of the world have been guests at the ranch and through the stone gateposts marked in wrought iron, *LBJ Ranch*, have passed the well-known and the unknown: presidents, ambassadors, astronauts, a camel driver from Karachi, and hundreds more.

Because it is a highly successful working ranch, each year 4-H club members and school groups pass through the gates to see the operation, and to hear ranching methods explained by the foreman, Dale Malachek. In addition, hundreds of friends have been there at various times as guests of the family.

One does not have to read the guest book inside the house to know the great and near-great who have sampled the expansive Texas hospitality dispensed by the Johnsons. They need only follow "Friendship Walk" around the house, leading to the swimming pool on one side. This walk is made of twelve-inch-square cement blocks in which the guests have signed their names and the dates. The cement is mixed and poured the night before into wooden frames. By next morning, it is firm enough to hold an autograph pressed in with a stick.

The Johnsons welcome foreign visitors to their ranch because it gives the visitors a chance to see what this country is like west of the Mississippi, away from the city lights and sidewalks in the East. They are glad for fellow Americans to come and see how highly developed and pleasant rural life can be, and to see the contrast between the Old West and the New West.

The LBJ Ranch is an authentic piece of Americana that retains in this fast-paced nuclear age much of the flavor of the longhorn cattle days of the West. Although the Johnsons have landscaped and terraced the front grounds facing the Pedernales River and the highway beyond, and have impounded the water by a small dam that spills over onto the only ingress road to the property, much of the LBJ Ranch lands could be rented out as background for a Wild West movie. Some of the land, lush with growing grasses—sudan, alfalfa, coastal Bermuda—that are particularly suitable to the very dry climate, and other crops, irrigated by water from the Pedernales River, could serve as a model farm laboratory for an up-to-date agriculture college.

Even the ranch house itself is a picturesque combination

of the colorful Old West and the emerging New West. Under the expert planning of Lady Bird Johnson, the original structure of thick stone walls has been transformed into a roomy, two-story house with snowy-white frame additions rambling off in all directions from the center in typical Western ranch-style. And every room contains all the charm and comforts that taste and the marvels of electricity can provide.

To one side of the house is a large kidney-shaped swimming pool, its water kept at a comfortable temperature by an elaborate heating system. ("We used to swim in the Pedernales River," says Lady Bird, "but after Lyndon's heart attack, we decided to splurge and build this.") The area around the pool is attractively landscaped and planted with a carpet of grass beyond the cement apron. Telephone outlets on all sides make it possible for the President, who is constantly on the phone, to discuss affairs of state or the local weather while neck-deep in warm water. Wafted over the scene is soft music spilling out of speakers hidden in the trees. White-coated servants scurry across the yard to the pool, heeding the commands of the master of the domain as the Johnsons enjoy a manner of living to which they have not always been accustomed, but one which they have earned by hard work and careful planning.

Turning off Highway 290 as it leads west from Austin, sixty-five miles away, a visitor may see through the gates a biblical-like scene: the Pedernales River (the name is Spanish and means "little white rocks shining in the night," Host Johnson explains), meandering through rolling green pastures dotted with fat, white-faced Hereford. Along the river banks are groves of live oaks that were there when Mr. Johnson's grandfather built the original house 103 years ago.

Scratched in cement in the President's bold handwriting at the beginning of the walk that leads to the house is

Welcome LBJ Ranch, and flying beneath the Stars and Stripes in front of the house are the Presidential flag and the Texas State flag when the Chief Executive is in residence there.

"This is where Lyndon comes to recharge the battery of both body and spirit," says Lady Bird, who likes to sit beside the swimming pool in the summertime and read poetry. But this is an indulgence she rarely allows herself. When she is at the ranch she takes on another role: that of ranch wife interested in all that is going on, including the new births among the cattle that roam the meadows.

Mr. Johnson himself partially sheds his official mantle when he goes to the ranch. He becomes a Texas rancher the minute he steps off the plane that lands on a $25,000 concrete strip a hundred feet or so from the kitchen door. Before he became President, the first thing he always did on arriving and the last thing before leaving was to get into a car or electric golf cart and go riding off to the fields to inspect his livestock. His pride and joy are the prize-winning white-faced Hereford and the Black Angus cattle which are sold for breeding purposes or consumed by the Johnsons after the animals have garnered an adequate collection of ribbons at livestock shows in the area. There are also Poland China and Landrace hogs, and Columbia sheep to claim his attention, plus half a dozen thoroughbred horses including a treasured Tennessee walking horse named "Lady B" after the mistress of the manor. Adding to the population of the private domain are half a dozen happy but useless dogs—most of them beagles—who follow his every footstep around the ranch, and two proud peacocks who let out intermittent eerie cries that sound like "'elp, 'elp."

Johnson's cattle inspections not only refresh his mind and exercise his limbs, but they also enable him to make judgments that affect the financial success of his ranching operation. Ranch hands say he is as sharp in the stock farm business as he is in politics. However, after he became President he placed the operation of the farm in a trusteeship that removed decision-making on such matters from his realm of authority for as long as he remains in the White House.

Although modest in size by Texas standards, the LBJ Ranch has become a show place and seems certain to become eventually a historic shrine that will tempt tourists from everywhere to the struggling towns in that area. It has not always been a show place, though.

When the Johnsons bought the ranch it consisted of 245 acres, a dilapidated house and few creature comforts. It had belonged to Mr. Johnson's eighty-year-old aunt, Mrs. Clarence Martin, and had been acquired by her father more than a century ago. Johnson bought it for $20,000 in 1951, trading a small house he owned in Johnson City as part of the deal.

"It looked like a haunted house in a Charles Addams cartoon when we bought it, and it is far from elegant now, but we love it," Lady Bird says. The original section was built in 1860 with the same thick stone walls that are found in the forts at Johnson City a few miles east of the ranch, which were designed for protection against Indian raids. This stone section today comprises the living room with its beamed ceiling and enormous hooded fireplace that holds four-foot logs. It was in this room that President Johnson held his historic talks with West German Chancellor Ludwig Erhard last December. It is in this room that guests gather for cocktails and conversation before dinner. In this room and throughout the house are reminders of the many interests of the versatile owners.

Shadow-box frames near the fireplace display a collection of Indian arrowheads gathered on the ranch, for this was once Indian territory. Hanging nearby is a framed copy of a letter written by the legendary Sam Houston to President Johnson's great-grandfather, George W. Baines, Sr., a Baptist minister in Texas and one-time president of Baylor University. History-conscious Lady Bird Johnson has often said that if the house caught fire and she could save only one thing in it, she would save this letter. It reads:

November 22, 1857
Huntsville, Texas

My Dear Brother Baines:

You will find enclosed your note and if you renew it for the same amount of $300 and send it to Mrs. Houston I will be obliged to you. You perceive that I knock off the interest for six years at 8 per cent per annum amounting to $140. This I am not loth [*sic*] to do as you have the luck to minister to congregations who think you can afford to preach to them gratis.

If you do not devise some plan to change their practices, they will think you ought to pay them for attending church when they could stay at home on Sunday and thusly be in greater readiness for the week's work. I am not alluding to charity though I think the scriptures enjoin that as one of the brightest Christian traits of character, and I allude to plain old-fashioned honesty of paying what they subscribe. They ought to know that paper currency will not pass in heaven. It must be the coin from an honest heart. Cotton fields and cotton bolls will find no market in Paradise. Mrs. Houston unites in affectionate regards to Sister Baines, yourself and family.

Truly thine,
Sam Houston

Furnishings in the living room include roomy sofas and chairs, arranged in front of the fireplace, as well as the

President's favorite chair, a rich tan leather recliner. In one corner is a permanent game table where Johnson plays a scientific game of dominoes (poor man's chess) with his friends as they discuss politics. "He is really good at dominoes and usually wins," one of them says.

Adjoining the living room is a small sitting room, which also serves as a library. Here the prized possession is a coffee table made from a polished slab of a fourteen-hundred-year-old tree from England's Sherwood Forest.

Off the living room on the other side is the spacious dining room with scenic wallpaper panels of a rural countryside interspersed with light blue walls. The tile floor is made of large brown and white squares, and in the center of the room is an oval cherry table which seats fourteen. One wall is a window that looks out on the rolling hills in the distance and, closer up, Mrs. Johnson's flower garden, where rose bushes bloom for nearly eleven months of the year.

Also on the first floor, with bay windows on the front of the house, is the President and First Lady's bedroom with a door opening onto a walkway to the swimming pool, where he likes to splash around first thing in the morning. This room is simply but comfortably furnished with a mahogany double bed, double dresser and rocking chair. A radiant portrait of Mrs. Johnson hangs on the wall facing the bed. There is a large walk-in closet for his and her clothes and extra shelves for his collection of Stetsons. (The big broad-brimmed hat has become one of his political trademarks, and several times in his Texas campaigns he has thrown them into the crowds in a dramatic gesture that always went over big.)

There are five bedrooms and baths upstairs, where guests—famous and obscure—have slept. When the Johnsons are at the ranch, these rooms are usually occupied and an overflow of overnight visitors comfortably installed in a cozy four-bedroom guest house down a short lane through the cow pasture from the main house. With all these facilities, the LBJ home is jokingly referred to as the "only hotel" for miles around. The guest house was designed by Lyndon Johnson, and some of their guests have liked it so well that they borrowed the plans. One who did was Minnesota Senator Hubert H. Humphrey.

Furnishings in the upstairs bedrooms of the main ranch house are homey and modest. On a high, handsome, old-fashioned brass bed in a dainty lavender-and-white bedroom is a lilac "sweetheart-pattern" quilt that Lady Bird's mother-in-law made as her wedding present.

In the downstairs hallway is the mounted head of a buck deer, whose antlers male guests use as racks on which to hang their broad-brimmed hats. At Christmastime each year Lady Bird covers the deer's nose with red-velvet à la Rudolph the Red-Nosed Reindeer, and hangs a green wreath around his neck. She also hangs a holiday wreath on the giant live oak just outside the gate to the house.

Guests are always amazed and amused at the vast intercom system connecting the entire house with the privately owned fleet of automobiles the Johnsons keep at the ranch, the private plane owned by Mrs. Johnson's broadcasting company, his three other ranch houses, his two boats, and the homes of neighboring ranch friends. Music is piped into every room at the ranch, and a loudspeaker in the large oak at the entrance gate pours out appropriate music for every hour of the day. Guests arriving at dusk may hear the mellow tones of Bing Crosby singing: "Where the blue of the night meets the gold of the day . . ."

While their guests are still breathless and starry-eyed from the charms and attractions of the ranch house,

Lyndon and Lady Bird Johnson pack them into a couple of air-conditioned Lincoln Continentals for a mechanized ride on the range. "Lyndon likes to have me and his favorite friends enjoy free moments with him riding over the country, looking at ranch land, watching the deer, or boating on one of the lakes," Lady Bird says.

These safaris on wheels usually take place after the sun goes down and the huge blinking stars begin to pop out in the distant skies. With Mr. Johnson at the wheel of one car and Lady Bird hostess-chauffeur in the other, they keep up a running commentary over the high-powered mobile radio units about the sights along the way. He always sets the pace, sometimes speeding up to eighty miles an hour on his private roads, across ranch lands, and Lady Bird gamely keeps up.

The President points out the deer, with their green eyes glowing in the dark, or turns a spotlight into the bushes to expose a doe with a baby deer looking trustfully at the intruder. Around another bend in the sometimes rutty road through scrub brush and boulders, as if on cue a buck bounds across the road into the bushes where he timidly turns to survey the scene.

Texas was still part of Mexico when Johnson City, a somewhat slow-paced but pleasant town thirteen miles from the LBJ Ranch, was founded by the President's grandfather, Samuel Ealy Johnson, as an Indian-fighting outpost more than a hundred years ago. Sam Johnson, who was born in Georgia in 1838, settled in the Pedernales Valley with his older brother, Tom, and bought land in Blanco County, Texas, before the Civil War. They built a log cabin and lived there for several years while driving cattle to Kansas, Montana and Wyoming. This was the first settlement on the site of what is now Johnson City and it was known as Johnson's Ranch.

In 1861 Sam Johnson left his cattle business to enlist in Company B, DeBray's Regiment, Confederate States of America, and served through the Civil War. He fought in the Battle of Galveston and had his horse killed under him at Pleasant Hill in 1862.

After the war Sam Johnson resumed his cattle buying and driving, and in 1867 married Miss Eliza Bunton in Lockhart, Texas. The young couple set up housekeeping in the cabin. Indians were still active in the area and two settlers were killed in an Indian raid near Cypress Creek in 1869. The President likes to point out the spot under the house where his grandmother hid during one of the Indian raids, thereby saving her life. He hopes eventually to acquire the house and nearby forts and commissary and to make them into a Texas historical center.

He hopes also some day to acquire the three-room frame cottage in which he was born. It still stands a half-mile down the road from the LBJ Ranch and until recently was occupied by a Mexican family. The President's mother, who died in 1948 at the age of seventy-eight, always hated for her son to point the house out because it had become so run-down since she lived there.

"It was not that she was ashamed of a humble beginning," explains Lady Bird, who greatly admired her strong-willed mother-in-law. "It was just that she loved her husband so much that she did not want people to think that was the best he could do for her. She used to say proudly that when she lived there it was always freshly painted, with flowers growing by the door."

Nearby is the stone-walled family graveyard, in which the President's mother was buried beside his father. Lady Bird personally sees to the upkeep of this quiet spot of beauty where ancient live oaks, some three centuries old, shade the graves, and purple sage blooms beside the gate. On a stone gatepost is a bronze plaque with a verse from Gray's *Elegy in a Country Churchyard*. It was a gift to the First Lady a few years ago from Elizabeth Carpenter.

When Mrs. Johnson drives guests across the fields of the ranch, pointing out the crops grown in each and explaining how the irrigation works, she always stops on a particular hill to let them view the peaceful pastures rolling down to the valley of the Pedernales, with the country church spire in the distance. "It is so pleasant on a summer evening to look down the valley and see that church steeple, and to hear the bells toll on Sunday," she says.

Another cherished "sight" she likes to show is the quaint little Episcopal church in nearby Fredericksburg, where she and the President attend services when they are at the ranch. St. Barnabas Church is a tiny, rustic log cabin with whitewashed walls and rough-hewn beams in the vaulted ceiling. It was originally a house built in 1848 by Peter Walter, an early German settler in the area, and was bought in 1953 to be used as a church.

There are only nine pews, each long enough to seat three persons, and when the President and First Lady arrive for the 8:30 A.M. service on Sundays, some of the worshipers move into the adjacent music room to give them a special pew. When Lady Bird was in Nicosia she visited the Church of St. Barnabas, built many centuries ago. She expressed a desire for some memento to carry from the original St. Barnabas Church, where the Christian martyr saint was killed after he returned to Cyprus with St. Paul to preach, to her little St. Barnabas Church in Fredericksburg. The archbishop of Cyprus had one of the ancient stones removed from the original church, and it was flown to Texas after an engraver in Nicosia lettered on the stone its place of origin. It is now displayed in a case outside the church.

A typical Texas treat—and one for which the Johnsons are famous—was offered to the United Nations delegates on their visit in April, 1963, as it has been served to other

VIP guests. That is a Texas barbecue, on the banks of the Pedernales River.

Elaborate preparations are made to present the prettiest picture possible on these occasions. Even the cattle are scrubbed down to look their sleekest, and the day before, ranch hands comb the area picking up every bit of debris and ordure on the green meadow. Mr. Johnson calls on their old friend Texas Barbecue King Walter Jetton to bring his chuckwagon down from Fort Worth to serve the memorable feast. At sunrise Jetton and his crew begin cooking the barbecue on a fire of mesquite and live-oak knots, and by noontime the meal is spread out on red-checkered tablecloths for guests to line up in ranch style and fill their plates. As appetizers there are barbecued ribs served with draught beer in huge tin cups. This is followed by barbecued beef, pinto beans, country potato salad, stewed apricots, pickles, onions, tomatoes, sourdough biscuits and deep-fried peach pies.

Topping off this spectacular show of Texas hospitality is a display of Texas talent that runs the gamut from a sharpshooting demonstration by a Texas ranger, to whip-cracking by a college beauty queen and sheep-herding by a Scottish border dog. Then there is always music—sometimes corny country style, with the special twist provided by a clowning combo called the Geezinslaw Brothers; sometimes grand opera by a soprano from Italy transplanted to Texas or spellbinding piano classics as rendered by Texas-born Van Cliburn.

Visitors to the ranch have not seen all until they have gone calling on the President's Cousin Oriole, an elderly relative and one member of the family that makes him sit up and listen. Cousin Oriole is really Mrs. J. W. Bailey. She lives in a little red frame house facing the Pedernales River, a short walk down the road from the Johnson ranch house. Her screened front porch contains a white iron bed on which she sleeps when the heat of

Texas is overwhelming and a cool breeze might blow off the river. It is also the President's favorite resting spot when he goes to call in the warm-weather months. His calling hour is often late at night. Just before retiring, he rounds up Lady Bird and whoever happens to be visiting at the time and escorts them on a moonlight (or flashlight if the moon is dark) stroll down the lane.

On arriving at the darkened house (usually she has already retired for the night), he calls, "Cousin Oriole, we've brought some people to see you." She quickly gets up, slips into a dress and comes out barefoot to open the latch on the screened porch door. Oriole, who recently admitted she is in her seventies, keeps her favorite cousin informed on the news along the Pedernales River, and with a little persuasion from him she will read his guests some of the poetry she has written on sleepless nights since she became a widow several years ago.

Once when she read her poems to Arthur Godfrey, he offered to take them to New York and have them published, which he did in a privately printed booklet. Now Cousin Oriole would like to get them set to music, but so far Lyndon has not brought to her front porch a composer willing to take on the job.

The Johnsons take their guests to other places in the area for sightseeing and entertainment. Among them are the three other ranches they own, all larger than the LBJ Ranch. All three ranch houses were decorated by Lady Bird, who likes to mix her own paint and sometimes wields the brush herself. These are furnished in early American maple pieces with many of the decorative touches provided by knick-knacks, souvenirs and gifts acquired on their travels around the world.

Some day the Johnsons plan to give each of their daughters a ranch, possibly as a wedding present, and it seems likely that Lynda Bird will have first choice. One ranch, which they call the Scharnhorst place, has 1,200 acres, which are used for cattle-ranging and deer-hunting. On it is a red frame ranch house with a cute front porch, on which ranchers of another day rested in the cool of the evening. Today, the house is air-conditioned, and inside are sleeping facilities for six or eight persons, and on the walls are the heads of two deer shot by the First Lady and Lynda Bird several years ago.

Several miles away, in a more remote but scenic spot, is what the Johnsons call the Lewis place. The little field-stone house here is surrounded by a white ranch fence with lilac bushes and other quite old shrubs growing in the yard. The home site is more than half a century old and the original house has been renovated and completely modernized by the Johnsons. Some eight hundred acres of ranch land goes with the house.

The third ranch house, the most beautiful of the three, is what they call the Haywood place. It was acquired as an investment with part ownership resting with Judge A. W. Moursand, a friend and neighboring rancher. It comprises 5,000 acres of land, with extensive water frontage on one of the artificial lakes formed by the lower Colorado and Llano rivers that flow nearby. Some of this frontage has been sold off as the site for summer homes, but the remaining lands are preserved in their untended natural beauty.

It is to this house the Johnsons come with their friends for a change of scenery, but they do not slow down the whirlwind pace that marks their movements elsewhere. Instead of deer-hunting, they indulge in water sports. A large boathouse at the shoreline shelters the President's two boats, one a cabin cruiser that holds more than a dozen persons and the other a speedy motorboat that skims easily over the water with half a dozen aboard. On the lake the President loses his identity as an important world figure as he cruises around, waving to passing boaters or fishing enthusiasts on the shore. Occasionally he docks to go calling on friends who have built weekend and vacation homes along the shore, and sometimes he takes a jeep ride through the hills to see fields of blue-bonnets or the yellow cactus blooms on the hauntingly beautiful landscape. These are the scenes that Artist Porfirio Salinas has captured on canvas, and that hang as reminders of home in the President and First Lady's bed-room at the White House.

[XIII]

From the LBJ Pantry

Probably the biggest argument Lady Bird Johnson and her husband have had in their twenty-nine years of marriage is over how much seasoning should go into the deer-meat sausage made at the LBJ Ranch. It is a good-natured argument that never ends but tapers off into laughs on both sides until the subject comes up again the very next time sausage is served.

Mrs. Johnson prefers the deer-meat sausage mildly spiced. The President wants his *hot*. When they make it to please Mrs. Johnson, he complains that he and no one else will eat it because it is not tasty enough. When it is made hot to suit him, she claims it is too hot for anyone to eat.

Whichever way they make it, they give a lot of sausage

away to friends at Christmas, birthdays, and sometimes on no special occasion at all but just when the Johnsons feel they have more than they can use. Mrs. Johnson likes to serve the sausage for late Sunday morning breakfast, with scrambled eggs, hominy grits, hot biscuits and boiling hot coffee. Sometimes she serves it as a late afternoon snack in tiny hot biscuits. Either time it is a sure topic of "hot" or "mild" conversation among both family and guests.

And just in case their guests find themselves with a deer on hand to turn into sausage, the Johnsons give out their recipe for making venison sausage LBJ Ranch style with an amount of seasoning on which they both agree. Here it is:

LBJ Ranch Deer-Meat Sausage

½ deer (ground)
½ hog (ground)
25 oz. salt
20 oz. black pepper
8 oz. red pepper
2 oz. sage

Mix together for 200 lbs. of sausage.

Nearly everything that comes from the Johnsons' pantry—such as the delicious okra pickles, which are a conversation piece at the First Lady's parties and which she gives in pint jars to friends, and the peach preserves—bears the label: *From the LBJ Pantry.* These labels have become collectors items and some people lucky enough to get a jar of pickles or preserves *From the LBJ Pantry* have been known to forego the pleasure of eating all of it in order to keep a half-filled jar on their own kitchen shelf to impress their friends and neighbors with the label.

President Johnson likes Mexican food and it shows up fairly frequently on the menu both at the White House and at the LBJ Ranch. He is a renowned chili fancier and has his own favorite recipe for making it. The recipe has been printed on 3″ x 5″ cards bearing a sepia drawing of the LBJ Ranch that are given as souvenirs to their guests at the ranch.

Although she is capable of whipping up a meal fit for the VIP's who dine with the Johnsons, Lady Bird does not cook any more and has not for several years. At the White House the First Family's meals are prepared by Zephyr Wright, and at the LBJ Ranch the chief cook is Mary Davis, whose husband works on the ranch. For official entertaining the Johnsons have French chef René Verdon, who was hired by Jacqueline Kennedy to spruce up the White House dinners and has been retained in this job by the Johnsons. In addition, there are four other cooks to lend a hand as specialists at various culinary arts.

It is Zephyr who is closest to the Johnsons, though, and knows just what to prepare to please their palates without any consultation with the busy First Lady. She admits she prepares what the President likes, and Mrs. Johnson and their two daughters eat what he likes. He prefers broiled foods and stays on a diet of low-calorie foods most of the time to keep his weight down.

After his first day in office, for example, the President went home to a dinner of broiled filet steak, spinach with marinated tomatoes, baked squash, biscuits and a jellied dessert decorated with frozen peaches. The Johnsons come from the heart of Texas peach country and the President has a special fondness for fresh-frozen peaches, often calling for a bowl of peaches—served without cream—as a bedtime snack.

Milk and buttermilk are the beverages at the Johnson family meals and the President usually chooses buttermilk. Instead of coffee, he drinks either tea or decaffeinated coffee.

Zephyr Wright was studying home economics at Wiley College in Marshall, Texas, her home town, when Mr. Johnson, then a member of the House of Representatives, asked the Wiley president to recommend one of his students to come to Washington as the Johnsons' cook. Zephyr got the recommendation and the job and she has been cooking for the Johnsons ever since. She knows what the President should and should not eat and follows the doctor's orders long after the President himself forgets them. She is an avid calorie counter—not for her own sake but his. And the low-calorie foods she prepares for him suit his daughters too, because they like to stay on a figure-slimming diet also.

Zephyr, who is married to Samuel Wright, an employee of the Senate, has an assortment of recipes collected by Mrs. Johnson from the days when she did the cooking. At the White House, Zephyr's domain is the new kitchen, installed in 1961 on the second floor of the Executive Mansion at the direction of Mrs. Kennedy. There she has a large stainless-steel range, a stainless-steel commercial-size refrigerator and maple-topped chopping blocks. These are almost identical to the equipment she had in the kitchen at The Elms, which was equipped under Mrs. Johnson's supervision.

The kitchen at the LBJ Ranch is facetiously called "Grand Central Station" because almost all guests arrive and leave through the kitchen, as the landing strip on which planes arrive and depart is only about a hundred feet from the kitchen door. The wallpaper in the kitchen shows photographers taking pictures of cattle, and world travelers bringing back the bounty of the earth. There is a tiny table that seats four in this room, and often the President and First Lady have a light breakfast together there if they have no guests. The kitchen is equipped with the most modern fixtures and gadgetry, including an ice-making machine that the President, who has a weakness for things mechanical, delights in operating.

Mrs. Johnson usually plans the meals at the ranch,

where diets and calories are forgotten. The flavor is always regional, and when she returns to Washington after a few days at the ranch she goes on a one-day diet to offset the sumptuous feasting that marks every meal on the ranch.

Breakfast rarely varies except for the fruit, and it is hearty enough to see anyone through a morning of hard labor or the strenuous exercise of roaming the ranch on horseback or on foot. There is an abundance of fresh orange juice and coffee immediately on arising, and at the table, some kind of fresh fruit, delicious slices of home-baked bread, scrambled eggs, spicy deer-sausage, ranch-cured bacon, and either peach, pecan or fig preserves.

Luncheon is apt to be a barbecue on the banks of the Pedernales River or a picnic served aboard one of the President's speedy boats cruising one of the artificial lakes that dot the scenery between the ranch and Austin, sixty-five miles away.

Dinner on Saturday night may include Southern fried chicken with rice and cream gravy, zucchini and tomato casserole, hot rolls, vegetable salad, ice cream and Texas pecan pralines.

Sunday dinner is no less caloric or delicious. That is the time for Texas steaks—thick, juicy, and grilled over charcoal—with creamed corn, marinated green beans, tossed green salad, hot rolls and pecan pie.

Thus stuffed on the inside from a weekend of meals at the ranch, no guest goes away empty-handed, for Lady Bird or her husband brings from the LBJ pantry a pound of deer-meat sausage, or a jar of okra pickles, or peach preserves to send the traveler on his way with a taste treat in store on arrival at his destination.

When Mrs. Johnson plans a dinner party in Washington, the menu is a bit more formal than at the ranch but original and full of the flavor of the Southwest. A year or so ago she gave a pre-theater dinner party for guests who paid $100 each for tickets to a benefit show at the National Theater in Washington. Everything was prepared from her own special recipes, and her menu was in the form of a playbill, with overture and curtain calls. This is the way her menu cards read:

OVERTURE

King Crab Meat   Noche Specials
Deer-meat Sausage on Hot Biscuits

ON STAGE

Filet of Beef   Fried Chicken
Mushroom—Lima Bean Casserole   Fruit Salad
Watermelon Pickles   Hot Rolls

Curtain Calls

Texas-size Brownies   Sand Tarts   Sugar Cookies
Coffee

A ladies' luncheon at The Elms would include all this on the menu: caviar, okra pickles, tomatoes, celery, quail, wild rice, baked pears, French green beans with almonds, broiled tomatoes, popovers, chocolate mousse and coffee. Mrs. Johnson has also repeated this menu with slight variations at some ladies' luncheons she has given at the White House.

Typical of the interest she takes in planning meals that will please her guests were her efforts last December to find something special for West German Chancellor Ludwig Erhard when he was a guest at the LBJ Ranch. She pored over old family recipe books and recipes of the area, and finally found a special recipe for Texas German chocolate cake topped with coconut-pecan frosting. She even searched out the history of the recipe and found that it had been brought to that area by early pioneers of German descent who had founded nearby Fredericksburg in 1846.

Here is the recipe she used, and also others from her personal recipe book. Included among them is a recipe for Double Divinity Fudge which is the President's favorite, and the homemade peach ice cream which they serve at parties both in Washington and at the ranch.

MRS. LYNDON B. JOHNSON'S RECIPES

Texas German Chocolate Cake

4 oz. sweet chocolate
½ cup boiling water
1 cup butter or margarine
2 cups sugar
4 egg yolks, unbeaten
1 tsp. vanilla
2½ cups sifted cake flour
½ tsp. salt
1 tsp. baking soda
1 cup buttermilk
4 egg whites, stiffly beaten

Melt chocolate in boiling water and cool. Cream butter and sugar until fluffy, add egg yolks one at a time and beat well after each. Add melted chocolate and vanilla. Mix well. Sift together flour, salt and soda; add alternately with buttermilk to chocolate mixture. Beat well until smooth. Fold in whites. Pour into 3 deep 8″—9″ layer pans. Bake in moderate oven (350°) for 30 to 40 minutes. Cool.

Coconut-Pecan Frosting

1 cup evaporated milk
1 cup sugar
3 egg yolks
½ cup butter or margarine
1 tsp. vanilla
1⅓ cups flaked coconut
1 cup chopped pecans

Cook and stir all ingredients except the last two over medium heat until thickened (about 12 minutes). Add coconut and pecans. Beat until thick enough to spread between layers and on cake. Makes 2½ cups.

Pedernales River Chili

4 lb. chili meat*
1 large onion, chopped
2 cloves garlic
1 tsp. ground orégano
1 tsp. cumin seed
6 tsp. chili powder (more if desired)
2 16-oz. cans tomatoes
Salt to taste
2 cups hot water

Put meat, onion and garlic in large heavy boiler or skillet. Sear until lightly browned. Add rest of ingredients. Bring to a boil, lower heat and simmer about 1 hour, covered. Skim off fat. Serves 12.

Noche Specials

8 tortillas
Fat for frying
½ lb. sharp cheese, grated
Jalapenas (hot peppers)

Cut tortillas into quarters and fry in deep hot fat until brown and crisp on both sides. Drain and put about 1 tsp. grated cheese and slice of jalapeno pepper on each quarter. Place in hot oven until well heated and cheese begins to melt. Serve at once. Makes 32.

Snappy Cheese Roll

¼ lb. sharp cheese
¼ lb. butter
1 cup flour
¼ tsp. pepper
¼ tsp. salt

Mash cheese and butter with fork at room-temperature consistency. Work in flour, salt and pepper. Form into roll in wax paper. Smooth sides with hand. Put roll in ice box until chilled. Cut thin slices and bake in hot oven (425°) about ten minutes, or until browned. Makes about 2 dozen slices.

Double Divinity Fudge

2 cups sugar
⅔ cup water
½ cup light corn syrup
2 egg whites, slightly beaten
1 tsp. vanilla
Dash of salt (added to egg whites)

* *The Johnsons use all or part venison, depending on its availability. Otherwise chopped or ground beef is used.*

Combine ½ cup sugar and ⅓ cup water; cook until small amount of syrup forms a soft ball in cold water (240°). Separately, cook remaining 1½ cups sugar, ⅓ cup water and corn syrup until it forms a hard ball in cold water (254°). Let first syrup cool slightly. Add slowly to egg whites, beating constantly about 1 to 2 minutes or until mixture loses its gloss; add second syrup in the same way. Add vanilla, and turn into greased pan. Cut in squares when cold. This candy is softer and creamier than the regular divinity. Approximately 40 pieces.

Texas Cookies

½ cup butter
1 cup sugar
1 egg
1 Tbsp. cream
Grated rind of 1 lemon
½ tsp. lemon extract
1½ cups flour
½ tsp. salt
1 tsp. baking powder

Blend together butter and sugar. Add the egg and cream. Add grated lemon rind and lemon flavoring to mixture. Add flour, salt and baking powder. Chill from 2 to 3 hours—better when chilled overnight. Roll out very thin and cut with "Texas" cookie-cutter. Bake 8 to 10 minutes in 375° oven. Makes about 3 dozen.

Spinach Parmesan

3 lb. spinach
6 Tbsp. Parmesan cheese
6 Tbsp. minced onion
6 Tbsp. heavy cream
5 Tbsp. melted butter
½ cup cracker crumbs

Cook the cleaned spinach until tender. Drain thoroughly. Chop coarsely and add the cheese, onion, cream and 4 Tbsp. butter. Arrange in a shallow baking dish, and sprinkle with the crumbs mixed with the remaining butter. Bake for 10 to 15 minutes in 350° oven. Serves 8.

Popovers

1 cup sifted flour
¼ tsp. salt
2 eggs, beaten
1 cup milk
2 Tbsp. shortening (melted)

Mix and sift flour and salt. Combine eggs, milk and shortening; gradually add to flour mixture, beating about 1 minute, or until batter is smooth. Fill greased, sizzling-hot pans three-quarters full and bake in very hot oven (450°) about 20 minutes; reduce heat to moderate (350°) and continue baking for 15 or 20 minutes. Makes 12.

Brownies

1 cup sugar
2 eggs
¾ cup flour
1 tsp. vanilla
½ cup melted butter
½ cup coarsely chopped nuts
2 squares Baker's chocolate

Mix all ingredients and spread in greased tin. Bake for 25 minutes and cut in 2″ squares while still warm. Makes 16.

Peach Ice Cream

1 qt. cream
1 pt. milk
3 eggs
1 cup sugar
½ gal. soft peaches, mashed

Make a boiled custard of cream, milk, eggs and sugar. To this, when cool, add peaches, mashed and well sweetened. Freeze. This makes 1 gallon of ice cream which is most delicious.

Spoon Bread

1 scant cup corn meal
3 cups sweet milk
3 eggs, beaten
1 level tsp. salt
3 level tsp. baking powder
Butter (the size of a walnut)

In saucepan, stir corn meal into 2 cups milk and let mixture come to a boil, making a mush. Add balance of milk and add well-beaten eggs. Stir in salt, baking powder and melted butter. Bake for 30 minutes in 350° oven. Serves 6.

White Bread

3 Tbsps. solid shortening
½ cup sugar
1 cup milk, scalded
2 yeast cakes dissolved in
¼ cup warm water
1 tsp. salt
1 egg, beaten
4½—5 cups flour

Cream shortening and sugar; add milk. Combine with the cooled yeast and, using egg beater, add salt and the egg, beaten until light. Add flour (1 cup at a time), just enough so that the dough can be worked by hand.

Put dough in a large greased bowl; grease the top part of the dough, and allow to rise until double in bulk. Cover with hot damp cloth several times. It takes about 2 hours for it to rise in a warm spot—not too near the stove.

Toss on board with enough flour to keep it from sticking to board; knead dough for 5 minutes, working outside edges in, kneading with the ball of the hand, repeating until dough no longer sticks to the board, is "bubbly" and puffs right back up. Divide into 2 equal loaves and place in two greased Pyrex baking dishes. Let dough rise again until double in bulk.

Bake at 450° for 10 minutes; reduce to 350° and bake for 30 more minutes. Bake until bread is brown and shrinks from the sides of dish. Remove and turn out to cool on wire tray. Slice when bread is cold. Makes 2 loaves.

Can be baked a day or two before—wrap in wax paper. It is delicious sliced, buttered and reheated.

Lima Bean and Mushroom Casserole

1 package frozen lima beans
1 Tbsp. butter
1 small can mushrooms
1 Tbsp. flour
½ cup milk
¾ grated cheese
1 tsp. salt
Dash chili powder
Dash of pepper

Cook baby lima beans in salted water. Drain thoroughly. Melt butter in saucepan; add mushrooms and sauté for 5 minutes. Add flour and milk to make thick sauce. Add grated cheese and let melt. Season with chili powder and pepper. Add lima beans and turn mixture into greased casserole. Bake uncovered (in 350° oven) for thirty minutes, and serve very hot. Serves 6.

Wheaties Coconut Cookies

1 cup shortening (½ butter)
1 cup brown sugar
1 cup white sugar
2 eggs
2 cups coconut
2 cups flour (or 2½)
1 tsp. soda
½ tsp. vanilla
2 cups Wheaties
½ tsp. salt
½ tsp. baking powder

Blend shortening and sugar. Add beaten eggs. Add coconut. Sift flour, soda, baking powder and salt together and add to mixture. Blend in vanilla and then Wheaties. Roll into balls the size of a walnut and bake 12 minutes in 400° oven. Makes about 3 dozen.

Prune Cake

½ cup shortening
1 cup sugar
2 eggs
1⅓ cups flour
½ tsp. soda
½ tsp. salt
½ tsp. cinnamon
½ tsp. nutmeg
½ tsp. allspice
½ tsp. baking powder
⅔ cup sour milk (buttermilk)
⅔ cup chopped prunes

Cream shortening; add sugar and eggs; beat well. Mix dry ingredients and add alternately with sour milk to creamed mixture. Add chopped prunes. Bake in 2 wax-paper-lined cake pans for 25 minutes at 350°.

Frosting

2 Tbsp. butter
2 Tbsp. prune juice
1 Tbsp. lemon juice
½ tsp. salt
½ tsp. cinnamon
1½ cups powdered sugar

Cream butter, add prune and lemon juice, salt and cinnamon. Beat in powdered sugar gradually.

Strawberry Ice-Box Pie

1 cool pastry shell	1 box frozen strawberries or 2 cups fresh berries, sweetened to taste
1 17-oz. package marshmallows	1 cup whipping cream
2 Tbsp. strawberry juice	

Put marshmallows in double boiler. Add strawberry juice. Cook until marshmallows are melted. Mix strawberries and marshmallows thoroughly. Chill about 2 hours. Fold in whipped cream to marshmallow mixture and pour into pastry shell. Chill until firm. (As a variation, add gelatin for *Stuffed Angel Food Cake.*)

One-Crust Pastry Shell

1 cup flour	3 Tbsp. cold water
2 Tbsp. shortening	1 Tbsp. sugar
1 tsp. salt	

Sift flour, sugar and salt together. Cut in shortening. Add few drops of water at a time. Roll out and fit in 9″ pie tin.

Apple Pie

Pastry for 2-crust pie	2 Tbsp. flour
6 Winesap apples	Juice of 1 lemon
1 cup sugar	1 stick butter

Peel, core and slice apples; place in bottom pastry shell. Sprinkle with sugar and flour that have been mixed. Sprinkle lemon juice, dot with ¾ of the butter. Put on top pastry shell, sprinkle with sugar and dot with remaining butter. Bake in 350° oven about 1 hour, or until brown. Serves 6 to 8. (Use above recipe for pastry shell but double ingredients to make top and bottom crust.)

Garlic Bread

Cut a loaf of French bread into thick slices. Spread butter mixed with chopped garlic between each slice. Put bread in hot oven for 5 to 10 minutes. Serve immediately instead of rolls.

Turkey Dressing

Medium-size pan of corn bread
4 slices toasted bread
Stock from turkey
6 eggs
1 stalk chopped celery
3 large onions, chopped
¼ cup melted butter
Salt, pepper
1 Tbsp. sage

Mix together toast and corn bread that have been soaked in stock from turkey. Be sure to use enough stock so that it will not be dry and stiff. Add eggs and remaining ingredients. Bake in casserole slowly for 1 hour, or until brown. May also be used to stuff turkey. Serves 8.

Chess Pie

2 cups sugar
1 heaping Tbsp. flour
½ lb. butter
4 eggs
½ tsp. vanilla
1 unbaked pie shell

Mix sugar and flour together; add soft butter and blend until light and fluffy. Add eggs one at the time, beating after each addition; then add vanilla. Pour into unbaked pie shell. Bake in 300° oven until inserted knife comes out clean—about 1 hour. Serves 6 to 8.

Cream Pie

1 cup sugar
2 cups scalded milk
½ cup flour or 3½ Tbsp. cornstarch
½ tsp. salt
3 eggs, separated
2 Tbsp. butter
1 tsp. vanilla
1 baked pastry shell

Mix ⅔ cup of sugar with the flour and salt; gradually stir in milk (save some of it) and cook in double boiler for 10 minutes, stirring constantly until mixture thickens. Stir the small amount of milk set aside into slightly beaten egg yolks; then gradually pour into thickened milk and cook about 2 minutes, stirring constantly. Add butter and vanilla and cool slightly. Turn into baked pastry shell. Cover with meringue made by gradually beating remaining ⅓ cup of sugar into

stiffly beaten egg whites. Bake in 400° oven for 7 to 10 minutes. Serves 6 to 8.
For *Lemon Pie:* Substitute 1½ cups of milk and ½ cup of lemon juice for all milk. Add lemon juice instead of milk to egg yolks.

Peanut Brittle

- 1½ cups sugar
- ½ cup water
- ½ cup white Karo
- 1 heaping Tbsp. butter
- ½ tsp. salt
- ½ tsp. soda (level)
- 1½ cups peanuts (raw or roasted)

Cook in large skillet until some of the sugar, water and Karo forms a hard ball in cold water. Add peanuts. Cook until rich golden brown, stirring all the time. Add butter, salt and soda all at once. Mix well, and pour immediately into buttered pan.

Spinach Soufflé

- ¼ cups chopped onion
- 2 Tbsp. butter
- 2 Tbsp. flour
- 1 cup whole milk or light cream
- ½ tsp. salt
- ⅛ tsp. pepper
- 3 eggs, separated
- 1 cup chopped cooked spinach
- ½ cup grated cheese

Sauté onion in small amount of butter and set aside. Melt butter, add flour and then milk, gradually; season. Add the sautéd onion. Beat yolks until thick and lemon-colored. Stir into white sauce; add spinach and cheese. Fold in stiffly beaten egg whites and turn into greased casserole. Set in pan of hot water and bake in moderate oven (350°) for about 50 minutes. Serve *at once*. Serves 4.

Banana Bread

- ½ cup butter
- 1 cup sugar
- 2 eggs, beaten
- 3 ripe bananas, medium size
- 2 cups flour
- 1 tsp. soda
- ¼ tsp. salt
- 1 cup sour milk

Blend butter and sugar; add well-beaten eggs. Beat in mashed bananas. Sift flour, soda and salt together. Add to above mixture, alternating with sour milk. Bake in moderate (350°) oven for 40 to 45 minutes in oblong baking pan, well greased and floured.

[XIV]

The First Lady in Action

When Lady Bird Johnson moved into the White House she said her role there "must emerge in deeds, not words." It was not many days before it became apparent that she would indeed be a lady of action.

If she had a private slogan as she took up residence behind the iron fence that encircles the eighteen acres of grounds and the 132-room mansion, it was "don't fence me in." She wanted to continue to come and go as she pleased, to be available to the friends, causes and clubs she had enjoyed and supported in the past. Even when her husband was Vice-President their telephone number had been listed in the telephone directory, and anyone who called was likely to find that the person who answered was the Second Lady. That is how accessible she and her family were to those who wanted or needed to get in touch with them. And she wanted to continue to be able to meet people from all walks of life, talk to them and know who they were.

Lady Bird had long felt that the government had paid too little attention to women, their needs and the contributions they could make to the country, and she often pointed out these facts to her husband. Thus, when he became President he was more conscious perhaps of the nation's woman power than had been any of his predecessors. During his early days in the White House he would teasingly say that Lady Bird always asked him when he came home from the office, "Well, what did you do for women today?"

She wanted to share her privileges as First Lady and her front row in history with the rest of the world. As a first step, she immediately began to let down the barriers that had been erected around the First Family's private life at the White House. She welcomed representatives of the nation's press, whom she regarded as the eyes and ears for people throughout the world, into the White House; not just to the state rooms on the first floor, but up to the private family quarters on the second floor which had been off limits to all except a few close personal friends and high-ranking foreign guests since the days of Franklin D. Roosevelt, when Mrs. Roosevelt held press conferences for women reporters in the chintz-decorated sitting room, and President Roosevelt held many of his conferences in the Oval Room.

At first Lady Bird and the President invited small groups—one or two dozen people—into the family quarters, and he very dramatically gave them the grand tour. Then, after she had been there twenty-one days, Lady Bird invited sixty women reporters, who cover her activities for newspapers, radio, television and magazines, for tea and to show off what she called "my own little private domain" —the family quarters on the second floor.

She received the ladies in the bright Oval Room, where a fire crackled in the marble-framed grate. The windows looking out through the colonnades on the South Lawn and the Washington Monument beyond were hung with sunny silk draperies, the walls were yellow, and the upholstery on the chairs and sofa was yellow cut velvet.

"In this room," Mrs. Johnson said, "John Adams and his wife received visitors once a week, and Dolly Madison was the first to do the walls in yellow—my favorite color. As you notice, over the fireplace is the porthole portrait of George Washington by Rembrandt Peale. Imagine naming a baby Rembrandt! This was a favorite room for President Franklin Delano Roosevelt; his desk was stacked high with papers, and after dinner he would see many off-the-record guests here."

Their master bedroom she called her favorite. It is painted white and has heavy damask curtains of French gray-green and white. Most of the furniture is white, as is the bedspread on the oversized double bed, and there is a telephone on each of the night tables at either side of the bed.

Next door is Mrs. Johnson's study, a Regency room with pale blue walls, and a window that faces south, toward the Washington Monument.

In the center of the west end of the second floor is the huge family sitting room, about fifty feet long and twenty feet wide, with a twenty-foot-high ceiling. A pale gold-slip-covered sofa is in front of the arched windows that continue to the floor, and other comfortable chairs are spaced around the room. In the center is an octagonal-shaped table piled with scrapbooks and photograph albums. In this room there is also a handsome mahogany secretary, attributed to the Baltimore cabinetmaker Joseph Burgess, and it is an outstanding example of Baltimore classical-style furniture at the end of the eighteenth century. Satinwood inlay is used in the delicate tracery of the glass doors and in the consoles of the pediment. Each glass door has a center oval of mirrored glass.

Lady Bird showed the family dining room where she now holds her ladies' luncheons. It was formerly Margaret Truman's bedroom but in 1961 Mrs. Kennedy had it converted into a dining room; the wall coverings are a version of the Zuber wallpaper "Scenic America" of 1834, except that this shows scenes of the American Revolution in the foreground, against the scenic background of Niagara Falls, Natural Bridge, Boston Harbor, West Point and New York Bay.

The tour led through Lucy Baines' feminine, ruffled, white-and-blue bedroom, Lynda Bird's yellow-walled bedroom, and the long hall that transverses the second floor. She pointed with pride to paintings of Sioux and Dakota Indians by George Catlin, on loan to the White House from a museum. "This hall is filled," she said, "with the furniture of great American cabinetmakers between 1800 and 1810, from Philadelphia, Baltimore and New York. History and furniture march side by side."

She led the note-taking newswomen to the rose-and-white "Queen's Bedroom" and stood by the canopied four-poster as she said, "To my mind, this is the prettiest room upstairs. Five reigning queens have slept in this stately but feminine room: Wilhelmina and Juliana of The Netherlands; Elizabeth, now Queen Mother of Britain; Queen Elizabeth II; and Queen Frederika of Greece."

The Treaty Room, with its massive Victorian chandelier that once hung in the Vice-President's office at the Capitol, and with the many treaties on the green velvetlike walls, is, Mrs. Johnson feels, "more a museum piece and less functional than the other rooms upstairs." She showed also the Lincoln bedroom, so named because it is now a bedroom and once served as his Cabinet room. On the mantel is a plaque: "In this room Abraham Lincoln signed the Emancipation Proclamation of January 1, 1863, whereby four million slaves were given their freedom and slavery forever prohibited in the United States." Here are a sofa, two matching chairs, a desk, two slipper chairs and a clock associated with Lincoln. Other furnishings came from White House storage.

Lady Bird used the occasion of the tea to give a boost to one of her husband's programs. She introduced as honor guest Mrs. Esther Peterson, Assistant Secretary of Labor and newly appointed assistant to the President on consumer affairs. Before the ladies took the tour of the family rooms, Mrs. Peterson explained briefly her program and the cooperation she is getting from "just plain people" who write her about consumer problems.

A few days later President and Mrs. Johnson gave the first in a series of informal dinners for senators and their wives. After dinner, while the President talked with the senators in the state rooms, Lady Bird took the ladies on a tour of the private family quarters. She remarked that she had never been up there herself until her husband became Vice-President, and she had often wondered before then how the First Family lived in private. She thought the members of Congress and their wives had a right to see. When the senators found their wives were getting the private tour they asked to be included.

A "doer" herself, Lady Bird planned a series of luncheons for other "women doers," affording them an opportunity to exchange ideas and talk about their work. Guests included women members of Congress and public officials, wives of members of Congress and government officials, distinguished women in the theater, college presidents and women active in various aspects of public and professional life.

There were fourteen guests at her first luncheon, among them actress Helen Hayes, Mrs. Philip Hoff, wife of the

Governor of Vermont, and Ellen Stoutenberg, director of the Hospitality Committee for the United Nations. Mrs. Johnson asked Mrs. Stoutenberg to speak at the luncheon, explaining her work in introducing United Nations delegates to various parts of the United States on "hospitality tours" to areas where they are invited.

The luncheons were always held in the attractive family dining room on the second floor. The second luncheon honored Mrs. Lester Pearson, wife of the Canadian Prime Minister who at the same time was a guest at a luncheon given by President Johnson in the State Dining Room. On this occasion, President Johnson and Prime Minister Pearson paid a surprise visit to Lady Bird's luncheon and each made a brief speech to the ladies. There were thirty-two guests at Lady Bird's luncheon, and they were served jellied consommé, pheasant supreme with wild rice, string beans amandine, broiled tomatoes, and strawberry mousse. The men downstairs in the State Dining Room had lobster thermidor, filet mignon Choron, O'Brien potatoes, asparagus polonaise, and strawberries Romanoff. Zephyr Wright prepared the ladies' luncheon, and French chef René Verdon the men's.

Shortly after she became First Lady, a reporter told Lady Bird she had been compared in many ways to former First Lady Eleanor Roosevelt and asked if she felt that she was like her. Lady Bird paused a long while, then answered earnestly, "I would like to be as good as she was, but I have no feeling that I am." Nonetheless, her character has an Eleanor Roosevelt quality, especially her concern for those in needy and depressed areas. This concern became more apparent when she decided in early January to fly to depressed anthracite coal areas of Pennsylvania to implement the President's campaign against poverty and employment. It is, she says, one of the things she likes most to do—meet and try to help people, to bring as much happiness as she can into their lives.

With a plane load of some forty reporters, she set out from Washington bright and early on January 11, 1964, for Scranton and Wilkes-Barre, Pennsylvania, to speak at the dedication of a new scientific research center at Wilkes College, in Wilkes-Barre. The center had been built with federal aid to lure new electronic and chemical industry to Pennsylvania mining communities hit by unemployment. She took advantage of the opportunity for an on-the-spot inspection of what is being done by the government, particularly through the Area Redevelopment Administration, to provide more jobs, and through the Manpower Retraining Act to retrain unemployed coal miners to perform them. And she also dispensed her own spirit of sunshine and warmth in the gloomy, snow-covered areas, bringing smiles to the faces lined with care.

She spoke to a crowd of nearly five hundred gathered to welcome her at the airport. She spoke before hundreds more on the snow-covered courthouse squares in both Scranton and Wilkes-Barre. She visited the Wyoming Technical Institute, where unemployed men are learning new trades, and a silk mill helped by an ARA loan, where she shook hands with each of the nearly hundred workers who came to work on Saturday in order to meet her.

"I have read over and over again the words 'depressed area,' " she said. "But I do not feel in the least depressed here. I sense a yeasty spirit. I sense that you are building your own economic bridge to the future."

Her democratic approach astonished and pleased everyone. She even invited the Pennsylvania state trooper who drove her limousine from the Wilkes-Barre and Scranton Airport and back "to come visit us at our Texas ranch." The surprised trooper, Donald Dorris, said, "You're kidding, Mrs. Johnson," but she insisted, "I'm really serious. The President and I want you to come down. We shall be delighted to have you as our guest." It reminds one of the time her husband impulsively invited a camel driver he met on a dusty road in Pakistan to visit him in the United States, and how delighted he was when Bashir Ahmad took him up on it.

Lady Bird got back to Washington at dark, just in time to make it to the White House, slip into another dress and take her place in the receiving line at a reception she and the President gave for members of the Democratic National Committee holding a meeting that day in Washington. "She's just back from the coal mines," her husband proudly told the guests as they shook her hand.

Later that night, she and the President flew by helicopter to Camp David, the presidential retreat maintained by the Navy in the Catoctin Mountains of Maryland, for a weekend of rest from what had been their busiest week in the White House.

On Monday of that week, her first day back in Washington after spending the Christmas holidays at the LBJ Ranch in Texas, Lady Bird and the President had given a delayed Christmas reception for the nearly twelve hundred employees in the White House and the Executive Office Building—from presidential assistants to carpentry aides. Typical of her acute perception, after shaking some twelve hundred hands, Lady Bird turned to an aide and said, "I missed some," and proceeded to name the employees who had not gone through the line. Afterward, she went into the kitchen and shook hands with those who had remained on duty during the reception.

Some months later she commented that she had enjoyed that party more than any she had to that time given in the White House because she had met employees who had worked at the White House for presidents as far back as Calvin Coolidge. She sometimes singled out certain ones to repeat the stories they had told her of how they happened to go to work at the White House in the first place.

On Tuesday of that busy week, she welcomed the labor

leaders who came to a stag luncheon, and the business leaders who came to a stag dinner with the President. She also took care of four house guests from Texas, mapping out sightseeing itineraries for the relatives of the President and herself.

On Wednesday, she attended the President's State of the Union address before Congress and praised his speech, which she had gone over after each draft, as "a pretty good synthesis of his living and working of the last thirty years." She said she particularly liked "the accent on education, on retraining the unemployed and on health. I liked the line about being strong enough to win a war and wise enough to prevent one." But the part she liked best was his opening sentence: "I will be brief—for our time is necessarily short and our agenda is already long."

That night, looking weary but willing to keep pace with the job, she accompanied her husband to a $100-a-plate testimonial dinner for their long-time friend, Senator Eugene J. McCarthy of Minnesota, who is seeking re-election this year. The Johnsons did not stay to eat dinner, but strolled among the several hundred who did, shaking hands right and left.

On Thursday she received workmen and donors at Blair House who had a hand in the restoration and refurnishing of the President's guest house where state visitors from other countries stay when they come to see the President; and on Friday she gave the tea for the sixty newspaper women.

It was indeed a busy week for a busy First Lady, and it provided an example of the kind of action the nation could expect from the new First Lady in the White House.

Lady Bird, a theater buff all her life, took special delight in combining her personal interest with a worthwhile project on a trip to New York in early January to attend the benefit preview of Arthur Miller's play *After the Fall*, produced by the Lincoln Center Repertory Theater at the ANTA Washington Square Theater in Greenwich Village. She flew to New York on an economy "air-shuttle" flight from Washington early that morning and spent the day visiting the Metropolitan Museum and the Whitney Museum. That night she was escorted to the theater by Adlai Stevenson, United States ambassador to the United Nations, and later went to a candlelit after-theater champagne supper dance in the Loeb Student Center on the New York University Campus. There she met and talked with stars of theater, politics and diplomacy.

Lady Bird's calendar was filled with other events in which she had a strong personal interest, as well as things to which she wanted to lend her support. She attended the exhibit of Vincent Van Gogh paintings at the Washington Gallery of Modern Art; gave a reception at the White House for four hundred college editors; with her husband, gave a series of six receptions for members of the House of Representatives and their wives; attended the annual Prayer Breakfast at Washington's Mayflower Hotel; was guest of honor at the Washington Heart Association's annual "heart luncheon"; accompanied the President to California for a visit with Mexico's President and Mrs. López Mateos; accompanied him to a Democratic dinner in Miami, Florida; and greeted the Houston Symphony Orchestra at the White House when they were in Washington to play a concert. She did all this in one month.

Elizabeth Carpenter, who perhaps knows the First Lady better than anyone except her husband, describes her as a "happy heart" whose "house will be filled with laughter, not just for herself and her family. She reaches out a hand, gathering people in to share her happiness and her window on the world."

That may be the key to the warmth and hospitality that flows out from the White House while President Johnson's Lady Bird is First Lady.